# RED HOT COUNTRY GUITAR

### By Michael Hawley

To access audio online, visit:
www.halleonard.com/mylibrary

Enter Code
2653-6476-2350-0486

T0055342

ISBN 978-0-634-07640-4

Guitar in cover photograph provided by Mequon Music.

HAL•LEONARD®

7777 W. BLUEMOUND RD. P.O. BOX 13819 MILWAUKEE, WI 53213

In Australia Contact:
Hal Leonard Australia Pty. Ltd.
4 Lentara Court
Cheltenham, Victoria, 3192 Australia
Email:  ausadmin@halleonard.com.au

Visit Hal Leonard Online at
www.halleonard.com

# Contents

# Introduction

This book is the culmination of twelve years of playing, teaching, and developing my particular style of country guitar. When performing, I'm often required to simulate the sounds of a pedal steel, banjo, or fiddle while maintaining the typical role of a guitarist. This makes modern country guitar a fascinating style to play and study.

All of this requires certain right- and left-hand techniques that may be new to you. Most of the examples in this book are played with a pick and fingers, or "hybrid style" approach. The remaining examples utilize the flat pick in an alternating down and up fashion. Many of the bending examples involve a certain amount of strength from the left hand and require you to listen closely so the proper pitch is achieved.

Learn all the examples slowly at first and gradually increase the speed. Pay special attention to the right- and left-hand fingerings provided. While there are several ways to finger these examples, the ones given will help reinforce the "licks to chord shape" concept.

Be patient and don't rush through these lines. Good practice requires focus, concentration, and repetition. I also strongly urge you to learn these licks in every key and on several different string groupings. A discussion of this can be found in Chapter 9. It's also very important that you listen to recordings and see performances by the masters of this style. The players discussed in Chapter 8 are a good place to start. Also seek out players in your own area and "pick their brains" about influences, technique, gear, etc. Most musicians are happy to share their knowledge with others.

Above all, get out there and play! Music is a language meant to be spoken with others. Playing in a group or with another musician is an essential part of learning to communicate through your instrument. I hope this book gives you some new ideas and insight into this eclectic style of guitar playing.

Enjoy,

—*Michael Hawley*

# About the Author

Michael Hawley is a central Florida-based musician and educator. He earned a Bachelor's degree in Guitar Performance from the University of Central Florida and is fluent in all styles of music. He currently performs throughout the southeast and conducts summer clinics in New Orleans, Nashville, and Connecticut. His website is www.michaelhawley.net.

# Hybrid Picking Technique 1

Modern country guitarists prefer a combination of pick and fingers called hybrid-style picking.

Place the pick between the pad of the thumb and the left side of the index fingertip. Picking is achieved with either a downstroke (⊓) or upstroke (v). The fingers are used to pluck, and in some cases mute ( ✗ ), the strings.

With the heel of your palm resting on the bridge of the guitar, place your middle finger (m) on the third string and your ring finger (a) on the second string. Plucking is achieved by striking the strings individually or together with the left side of the middle (m) or ring (a) fingertips. Keep your wrist flat and let the fingers follow through into your palm.

Here is a good exercise that utilizes the hybrid technique. Follow right- and left-hand fingerings carefully and let all notes ring out.

TRACK 1

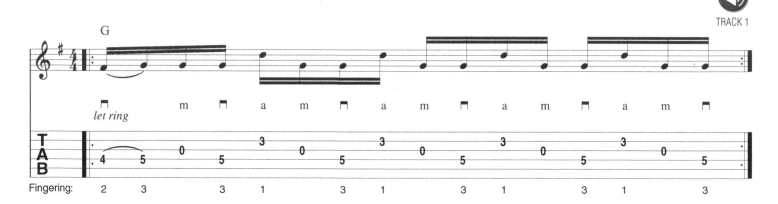

Notice the slur or *hammer-on* in beat 1. This technique is achieved by picking the first note, then hammering down the specified finger to sound the next note.

## Banjo Rolls

In the next example, continue the right-hand fingering while switching chords with the left. This produces a jangly banjo-like sound common in country music. Notice the *slides* in the second and fourth measures. These are accomplished by picking the first note and sliding your left-hand finger to the next note without picking it. This technique allows a smooth shift (position change) up or down the neck.

TRACK 2

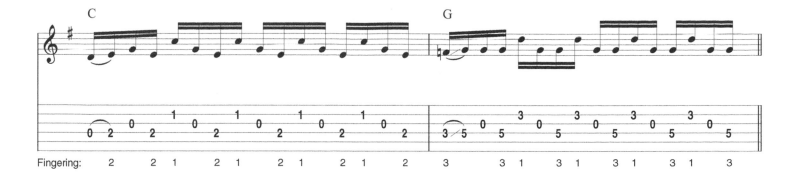

## Chicken Pickin'

Hybrid picking technique is often used when playing single notes (one string) or double stops (two strings played together). Single notes are played by alternating the middle (m) finger and a downstroke (⊓) of the pick. Double stops are achieved by plucking with the ring (a) and middle (m) fingers together.

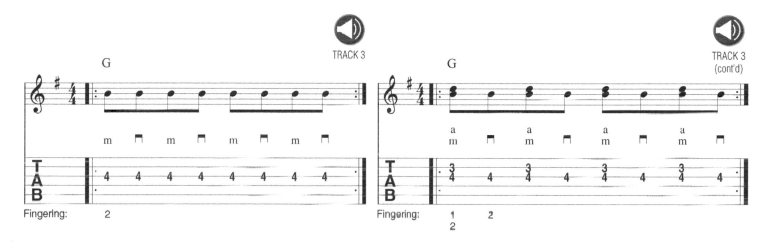

Muting every other note produces a percussive effect common in country guitar and similar to the sound of a chicken clucking; this is where the technique derives its name. Place the middle finger (m) on the G string to mute it. Play a downstroke (⊓) with the pick, then follow through with an unmuted (m) and/or (a).

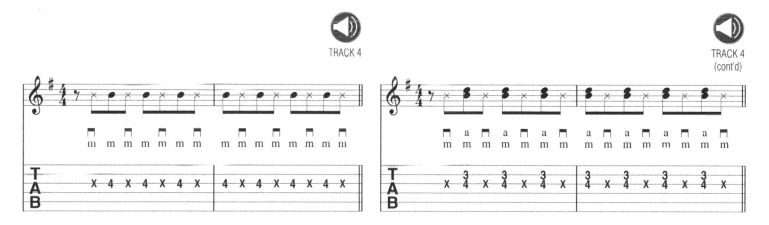

Pull the strings hard with your right-hand fingers so they slap against the frets!

# Country Rhythm Technique

Although simple strumming patterns can be applied to chord progressions, many country guitarists prefer to use hybrid picking for rhythm playing. This gives a clearer definition between bass and treble portions of a chord. It also allows for separate rhythmic and melodic lines to be played simultaneously.

The following example demonstrates how a country guitarist might play a progression in the key of G major. Note the use of simple open-position chords and the presence of the root on beats 1, 2, 3, and 4. Hammer-ons are also employed throughout to embellish the basic chord shapes.

# Single-Note Soloing

## Major Pentatonic Scales in Position

The most important scale in country guitar is the major pentatonic. Below are four common fingerings for the scale in second position. Position is determined by the fret being played by your first finger. In the following examples, your first finger is over the second fret. This indicates second position and includes frets 2, 3, 4, and 5. These frets are played with the first, second, third, and fourth fingers, respectively.

Notice the open circles below the root in each diagram. When playing scales in position, start on the root and ascend. When descending, play all notes below the root before ascending back to the root.

**C Major Pentatonic**

**G Major Pentatonic**

**D Major Pentatonic**

**A Major Pentatonic**

# Sliding Major Pentatonic Scales

Scales can be played along the length of the neck as well. Below are two fingerings that cover the majority of the fretboard. Form 1 has its root on the sixth string and spans nearly three octaves of G major pentatonic. Form 2 has its root on the fifth string and spans a little more than two octaves of C major pentatonic. Position shifts occur with the second and third fingers when ascending and the first finger when descending. Both forms are written here in ascending and descending versions. Arrows indicate position shifts up and down the neck. Follow the left-hand fingerings closely and strive for a smooth and connected sound.

**ascending**          **Form 1 – G Major Pentatonic**          **descending**

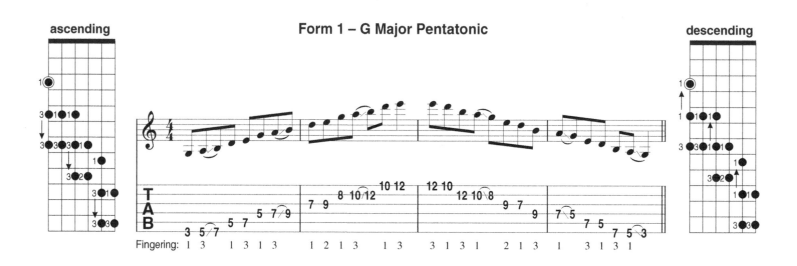

Fingering:  1  3    1  3  1  3    1  2  1  3    1  3    3  1  3  1    2  1  3    1    3  1  3  1

**ascending**          **Form 2 – C Major Pentatonic**          **descending**

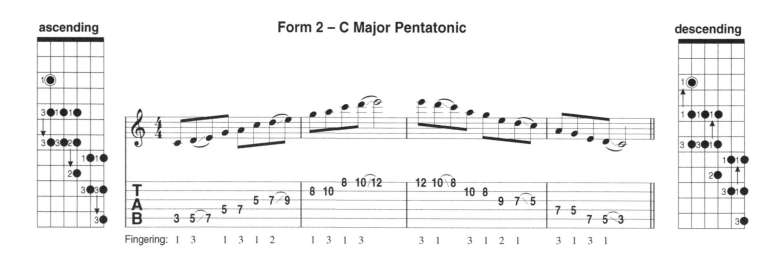

Fingering:  1  3    1  3  1  2    1  3  1  3    3  1    3  1  2  1    3  1  3  1

# Minor Pentatonic Scales

## The Relative Minor Concept

For every major scale, there is a related minor scale that consists of the same notes. It can be found by going to the sixth scale degree of the major scale, or three frets down on the guitar. In the major pentatonic, the first note below the root is a distance of three frets. By treating this as our new root, we generate the relative minor pentatonic. This is a very important concept when soloing. Following are the four major pentatonic scales discussed earlier. Each has been transformed into its corresponding relative minor.

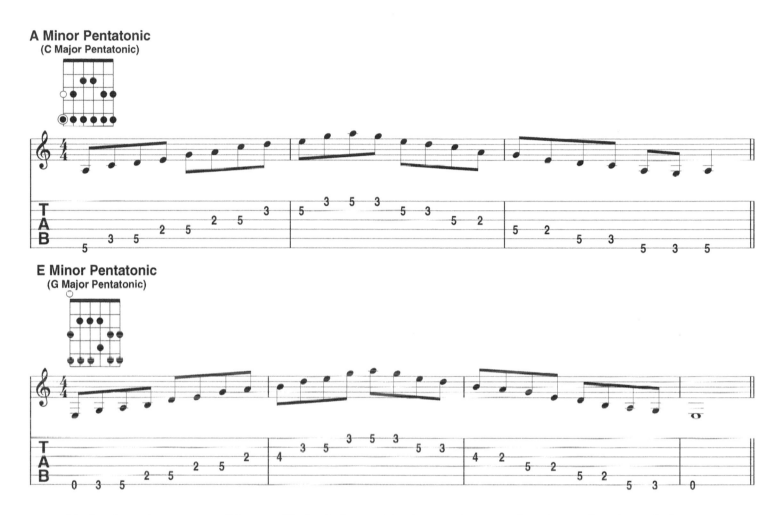

Notice that whenever possible we still play below and back up to the root when descending through the scale.

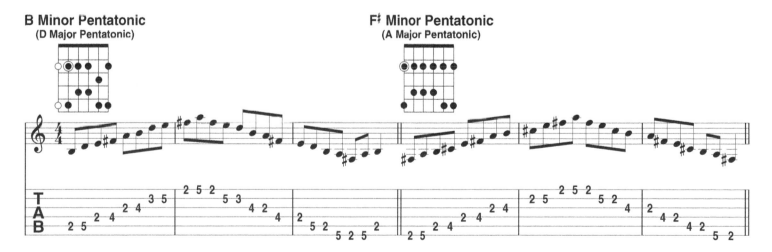

Transform your sliding major pentatonic forms into relative minors as well. Form 1 of G major would become E minor pentatonic and would begin on the open sixth string. Form 2 of C major pentatonic would become A minor pentatonic and begin with the third finger on the fifth fret of the sixth string.

## The Relative Major Concept

By starting on the first note above the root of the minor pentatonic, we generate our original major pentatonic scales. Each of these is shown in parentheses below its related minor in the preceding diagrams. This concept is known as relative major and is simply relative minor in reverse.

## Pentatonic Scale Applications

Let's look at three common soloing applications of pentatonic scales.

1.  Match the major pentatonic scale with the key of the song. For example, use G major pentatonic over primary chords in the key of G (G, C, D, and Em).

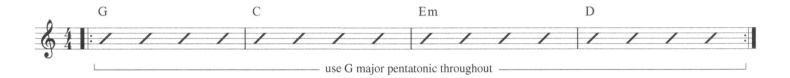

2.  Switch scales at the same rate as the chords. For example play C major pentatonic over C, then F major pentatonic over F, and G major pentatonic over G or G7. Because A is the relative minor of C major, use C major pentatonic over Am.

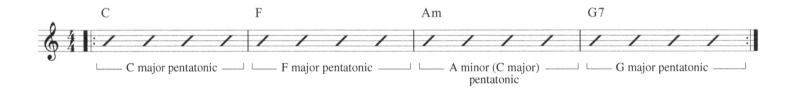

3.  Match the relative minor pentatonic with a 12-bar blues in the same key. For example use A minor (C major pentatonic) over A, D, and E or E7 chords.

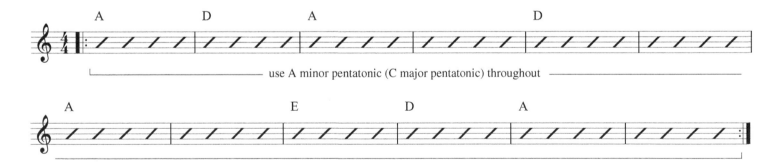

# The Blues Scale and Chromaticism

Adding one new note to the minor pentatonic produces another very popular scale in country guitar known as the *blues scale*. Unlike the major and minor pentatonic, the blues scale contains chromaticism. Chromaticism is defined as any note or chord that moves in half steps. On the guitar a half step is most easily seen as a one-fret distance in either direction on the same string. If you look closely at the pentatonic scales in this chapter you'll discover none of them contain any half steps. This exclusion adds to the openness of their sound and is the primary reason why they work over such a variety of chords and progressions.

When introducing chromatic notes into pentatonic scales, the variety of chords and progressions they'll work over is reduced. However, with chromatics comes a more sophisticated and colorful sound. For example, the tone being added to the minor pentatonic scales below is often referred to as the "blue note."

In each example, the added chromatic notes are shown in parentheses.

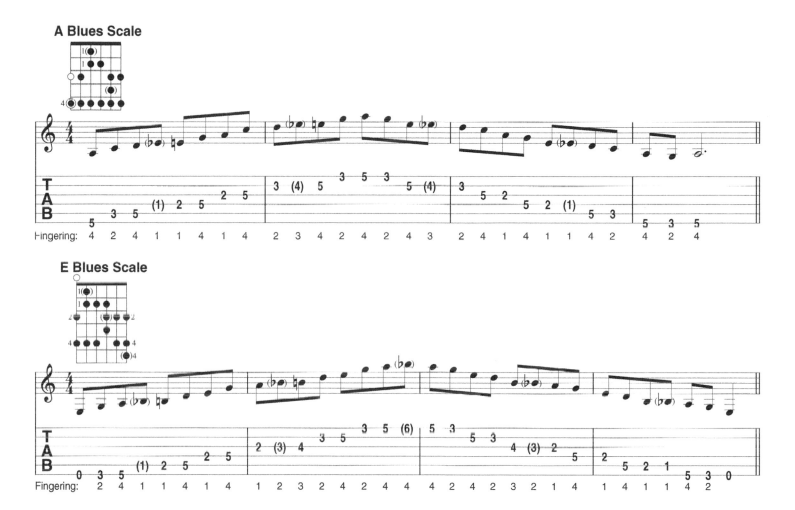

Note the use of first- and fourth-finger shifts in many of these examples.

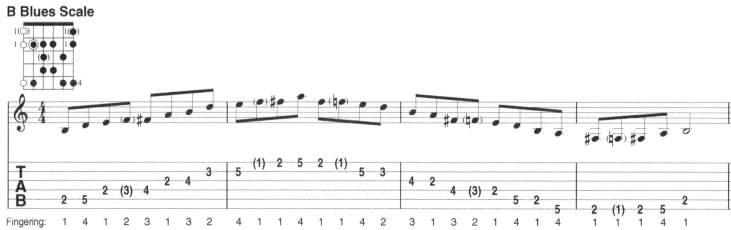

## F♯ Blues Scale

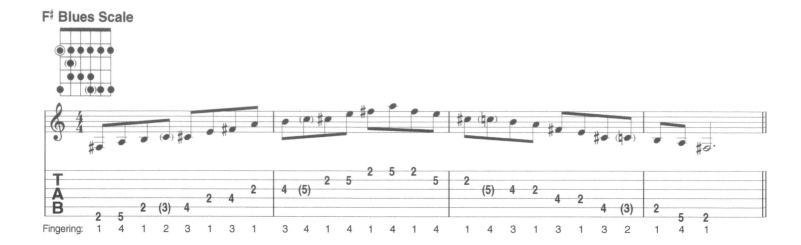

Fingering:  1  4  1  2  3  1  3  1    3  4  1  4  1  4  1  4    1  4  3  1  3  1  3  2    1  4  1

## Open-Position Blues Scales

It is common for both the E and A blues scales to be played in open position. The combination of fretted and open strings adds to the characteristic country twang. Below are the two most popular fingerings.

### E Blues Scale
(open position)

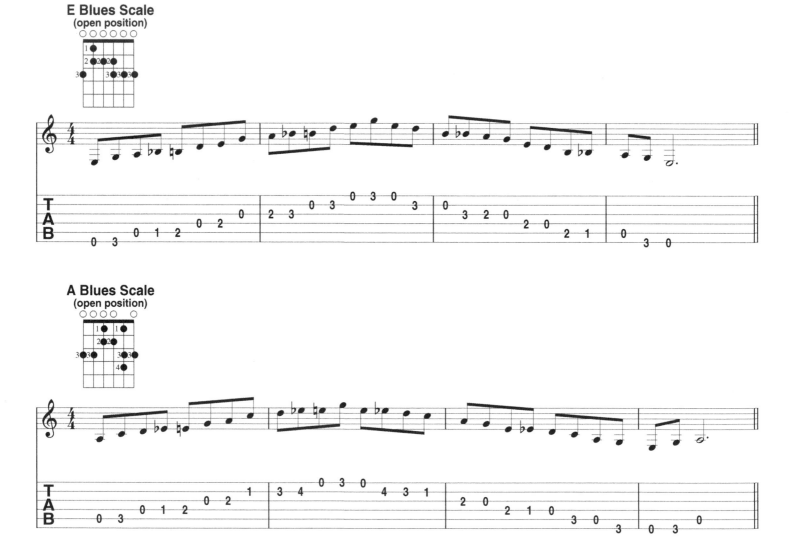

### A Blues Scale
(open position)

# The Country Composite Scale

By applying the relative major concept to the blues scale (starting one note above the root) we generate the country composite scale. This scale can also be viewed as a major pentatonic with one added chromatic tone: the minor third.

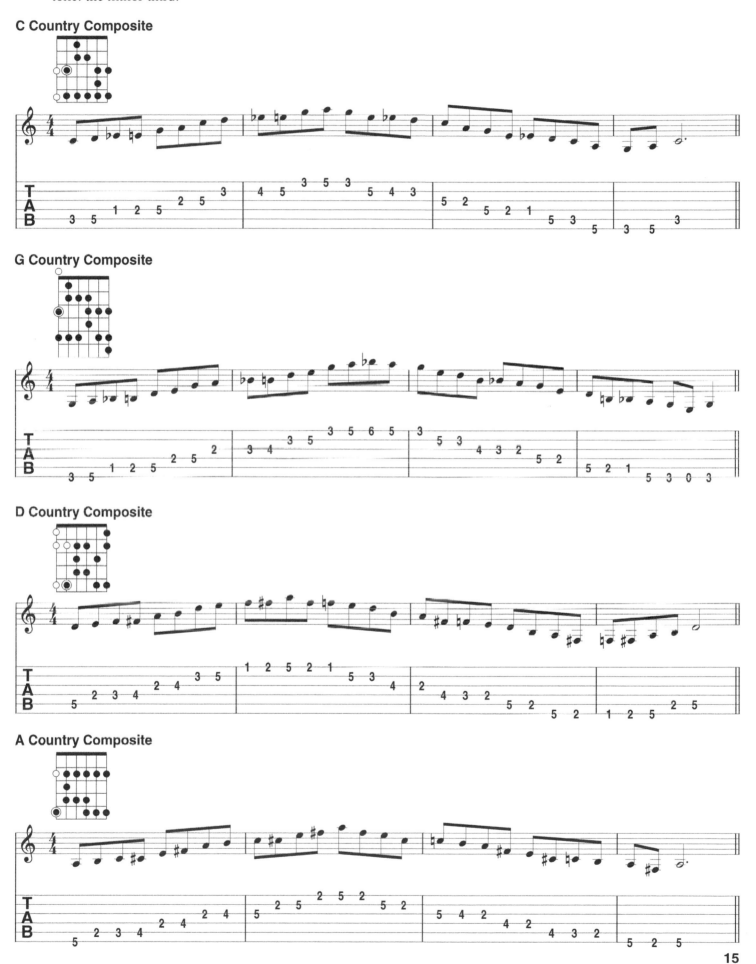

## Open-Position Country Composite Scales

It is common for the G and C country composite scales to be played in open position. The mixture of open and fretted notes is an important ingredient in giving your single-note lines that country twang. Below are the two most popular fingerings.

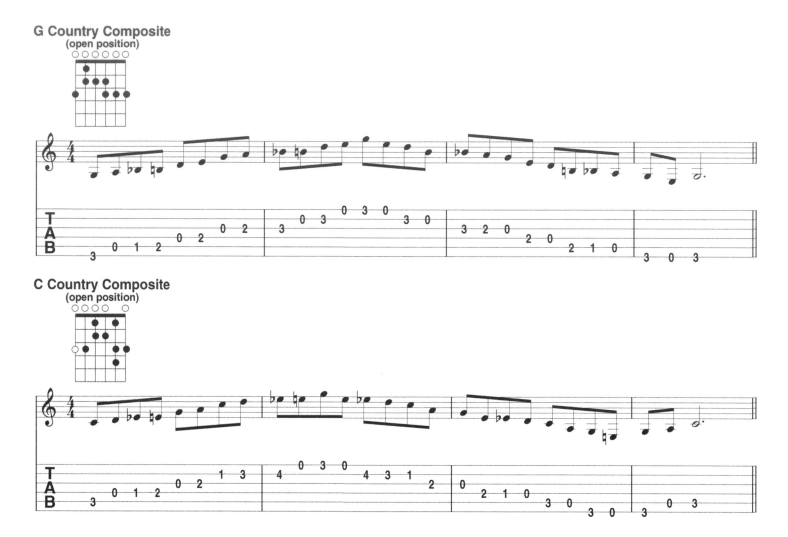

# Improvising with the Country Composite Scale and the Blues Scale

When improvising with the country composite and blues scale, the added chromatic note should be viewed as a passing tone. Passing tones are approached and left by a half step (one fret) in the same direction and generally occur on weak beats. The following lines illustrate this concept.

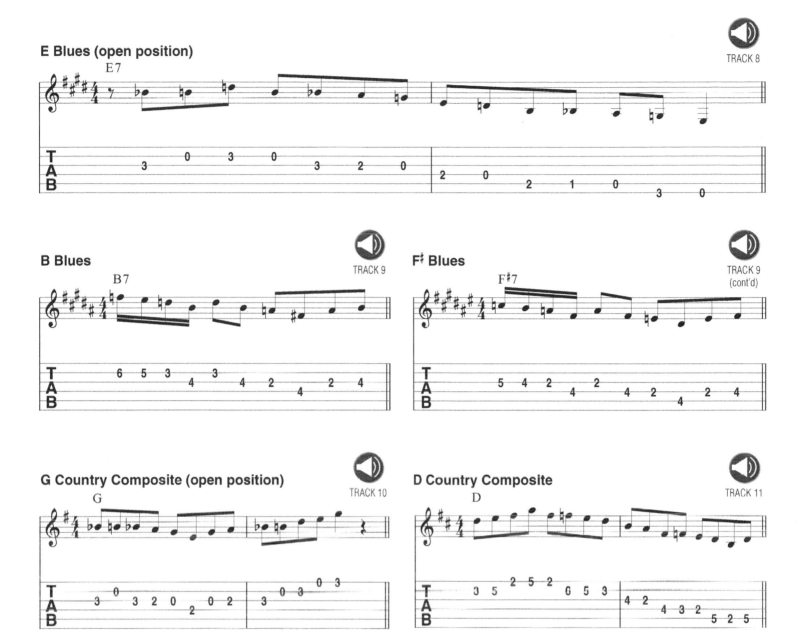

**E Blues (open position)**

TRACK 8

E7

**B Blues**

TRACK 9

B7

**F# Blues**

TRACK 9 (cont'd)

F#7

**G Country Composite (open position)**

TRACK 10

G

**D Country Composite**

TRACK 11

D

# Open-Chord Licks

## The CAGED System

While the composite and major pentatonic are essential to country guitar, single-note soloing requires the use of more than these two scales. It is common to generate a series of melodic ideas based on familiar and recurring chord shapes. These different melodic ideas are called *licks* and often change with chords in a song. These licks can be strung together and manipulated to create a cohesive solo. We will focus on licks based on five common chord shapes. This is known as the CAGED system.

The CAGED system refers to the five open-position major chords shown below. By visualizing each shape we can create and store a wealth of licks and ideas. These shapes can then be used like a roadmap to navigate our way from one chord to the next in the course of a song.

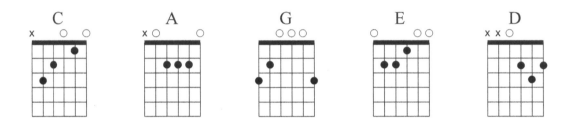

## Ascending Open-Chord Form Licks

The following examples demonstrate some simple licks over each of the five chord forms. Use the flatpick and remember to alternate down-up (⊓-∨).Unless otherwise notated, use one finger per fret (i.e. first finger/first fret, second finger/second fret, etc.).

TRACK 12

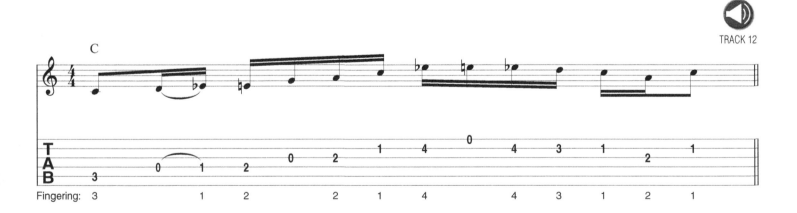

Play the corresponding major chord before and after each lick. This will help you hear and see the structure of each. Beat 3 of the next example uses a *pull-off* technique. This is essentially the opposite of the hammer-on we saw earlier.

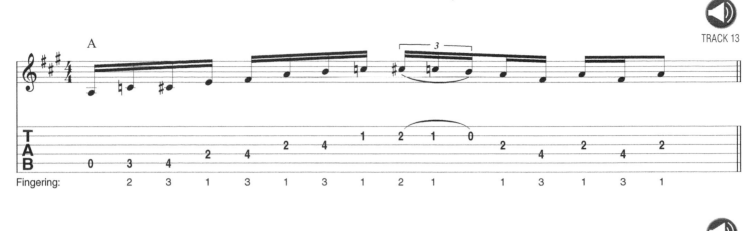

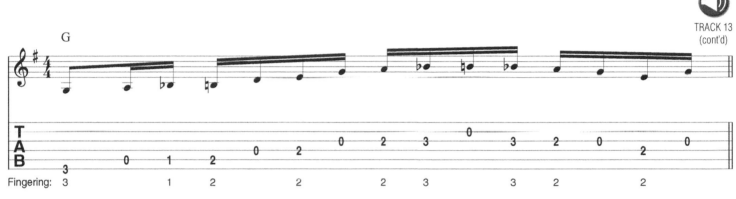

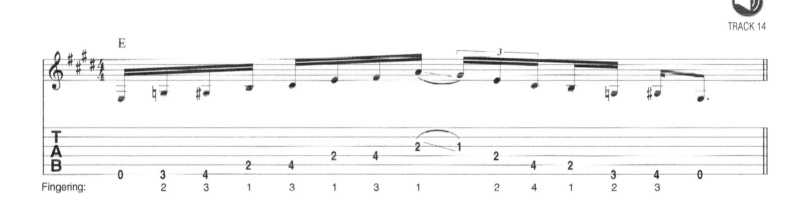

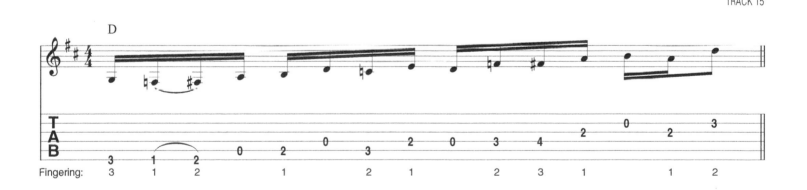

# Descending Open-Chord Form Licks

Here are descending licks over the same five chord forms in the CAGED system. Remember to visualize the shape of each chord as you play these!

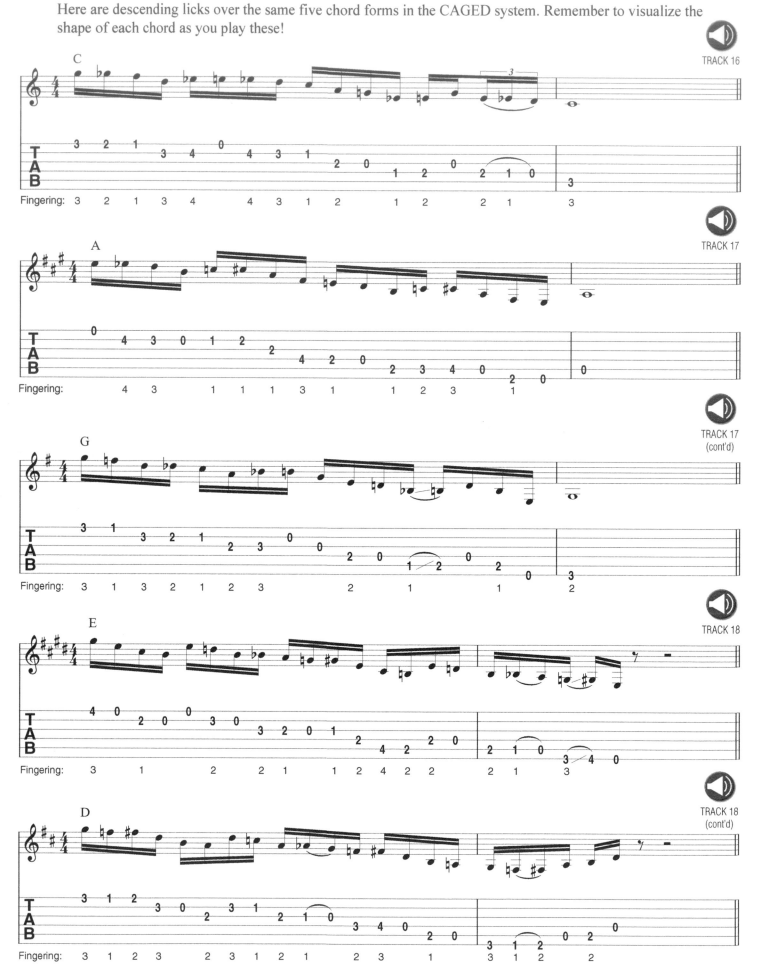

Note the use of hammer-ons, pull-offs, and slides. These give the licks a smooth and connected feel.

## Chord Progression for Single-Note Solo

Here is a typical progression in G major. Roman numerals track chord movement throughout the key. Pick downstrokes on single notes and strum down-up on the chords. When accompanying a soloist in country or bluegrass, the combination of bass notes and strumming is extremely common.

# Sample Solo in Open Position

The following shows our I–IV–V progression with the licks included. Note the use of both ascending and descending lines that smoothly connect one lick to another.

If you begin with an ascending line, the next should descend. If you start with a descending lick, follow with one that ascends. This will give your solo a strong melodic contour and allow you to stay within one position on the fretboard.

TRACK 19

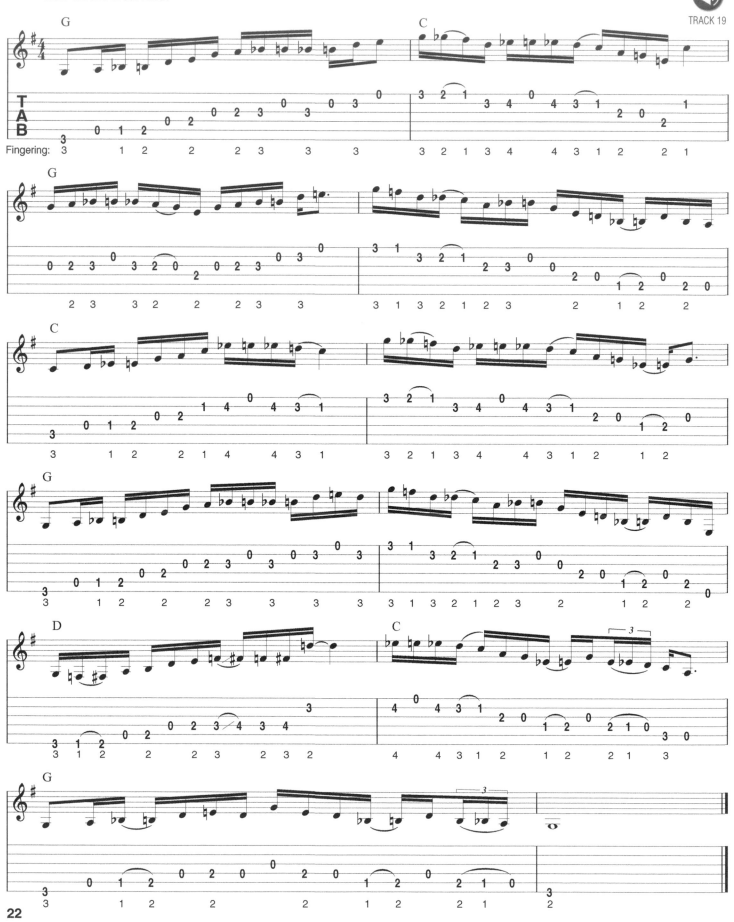

22

The majority of these licks were taken verbatim from earlier examples. But in some cases they have been slightly altered to fit over the given chord and progression. Licks are commonly altered by: 1) changing the rhythm, 2) repeating a portion, or 3) playing only a portion. Manipulating licks in this manner is essential to developing a strong single-note lead style.

## Open-Position Solo: "Doc"

We'll conclude this chapter with a composition of mine based on open-string licks. It was inspired by the great bluegrass guitarist Doc Watson, and contains many of the lines reviewed in this chapter.

TRACK 20

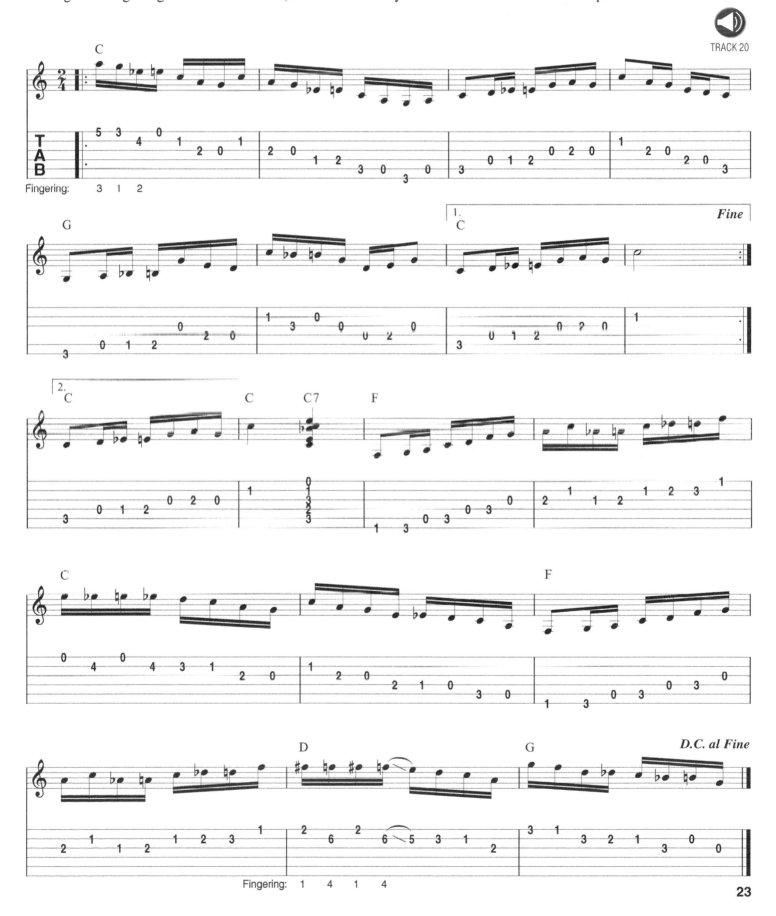

# Movable Chord Licks

## Closed-Position Movable Forms

The CAGED system can be applied to movable chord forms as well. Movable forms, or barre chords, contain no open strings, and are thus sometimes referred to as "closed-position" chord forms. They retain the same shape and fingering in any position on the neck. Sliding the original five open chords two frets up generates the following movable barre chords. Note that the first finger barres across the second fret, taking the place of the nut in the open-chord version. The original open chord is shown in parentheses below each diagram.

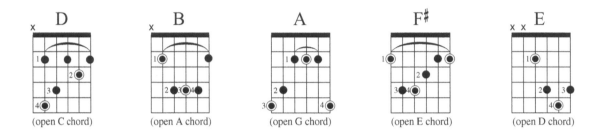

| D | B | A | F# | E |
|---|---|---|----|---|
| (open C chord) | (open A chord) | (open G chord) | (open E chord) | (open D chord) |

## Licks Surrounding Movable Forms

The following examples demonstrate some licks over each of the five movable chord forms. All examples are in second position unless otherwise notated. Practice each line slowly, taking note of where position shifts and slides occur. Like the open-chord licks, play the corresponding barre chord before and after each line.

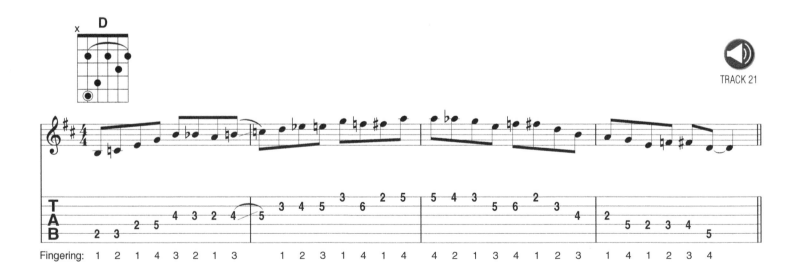

TRACK 21

Fingering:  1  2  1  4  3  2  1  3    1  2  3  1  4  1  4    4  2  1  3  4  1  2  3    1  4  1  2  3  4

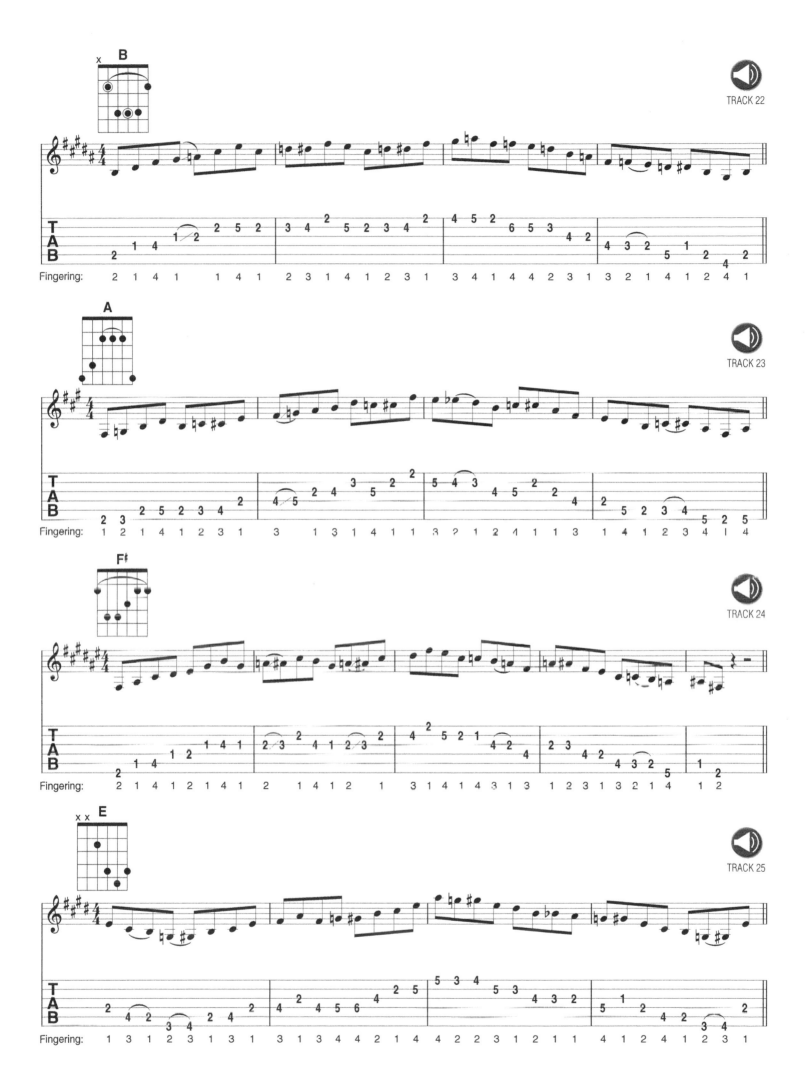

# Mapping the Fretboard with Closed-Position Forms

With closed-position forms we can map out I, IV, and V chords in any key. This is achieved by locating the root of each chord and visualizing the resulting fretboard pattern. Below are two common patterns for the I, IV, and V chords. Roman numerals indicate the root. From this we can use one of the five closed-position shapes to build the necessary chord. The keys are shown above each diagram and the resulting chord fingerings are shown below.

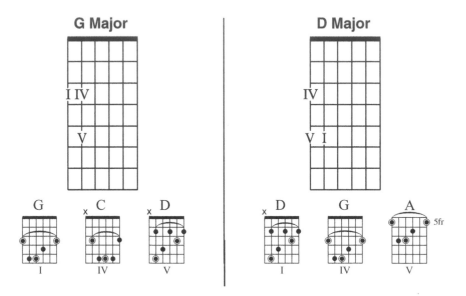

Closed-position shapes are also useful when mapping out several positions for the same chord. Below is an ascending line in A major that covers the entire length of the fretboard. The diagrams show each of the five chord forms being used as the lick works its way up the neck. Notice that, as in the sliding major pentatonic scales, most of the position shifts occur with the second or third fingers.

TRACK 26

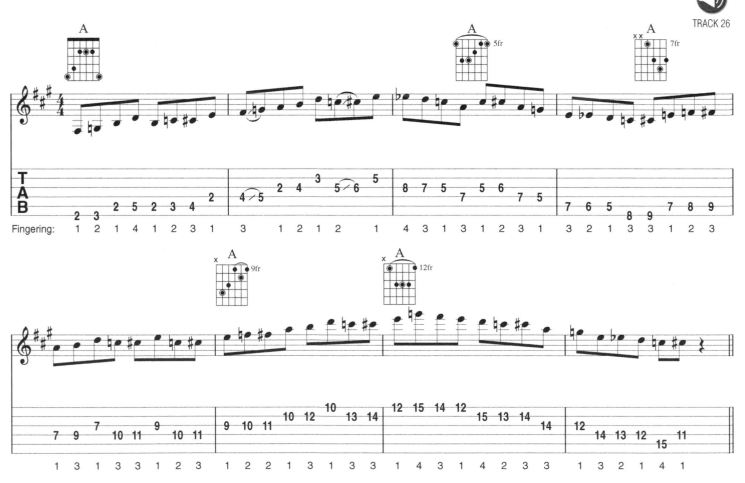

# Sample Solo Based on Movable Chord Forms

The following is a typical progression in A major. Roman numerals track the movement throughout the key. Notice the B7 chord in measures 13 and 14. This is an example of secondary dominant harmony. Secondary dominant chords are taken from outside the key and embellish typical I, IV, V progressions. In the following example B7 is seen as the V7 chord in the key of E major. Because E major is a 5th away from A, B7 is analyzed as V7/V. This type of chord movement is extremely common in country music. Play the following progression with the open-position chords shown and strum down-up on the eighth notes.

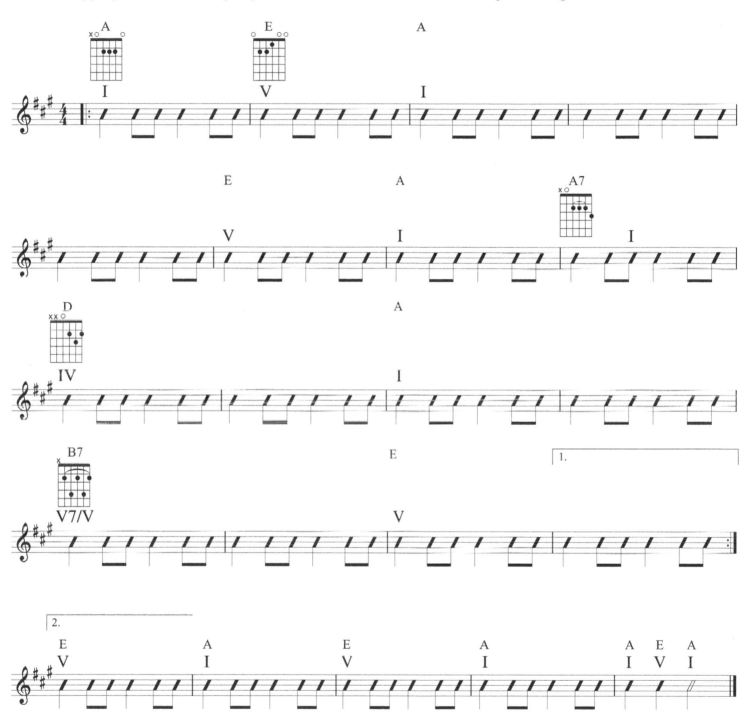

The following solo demonstrates closed-position licks over our chord progression in A major. The diagrams above the staff indicate which shape is being used. It is very important to visualize these chord shapes and hear how they relate to the structure of each melodic line. Follow the left-hand fingering carefully, taking note of how the position shifts are achieved.

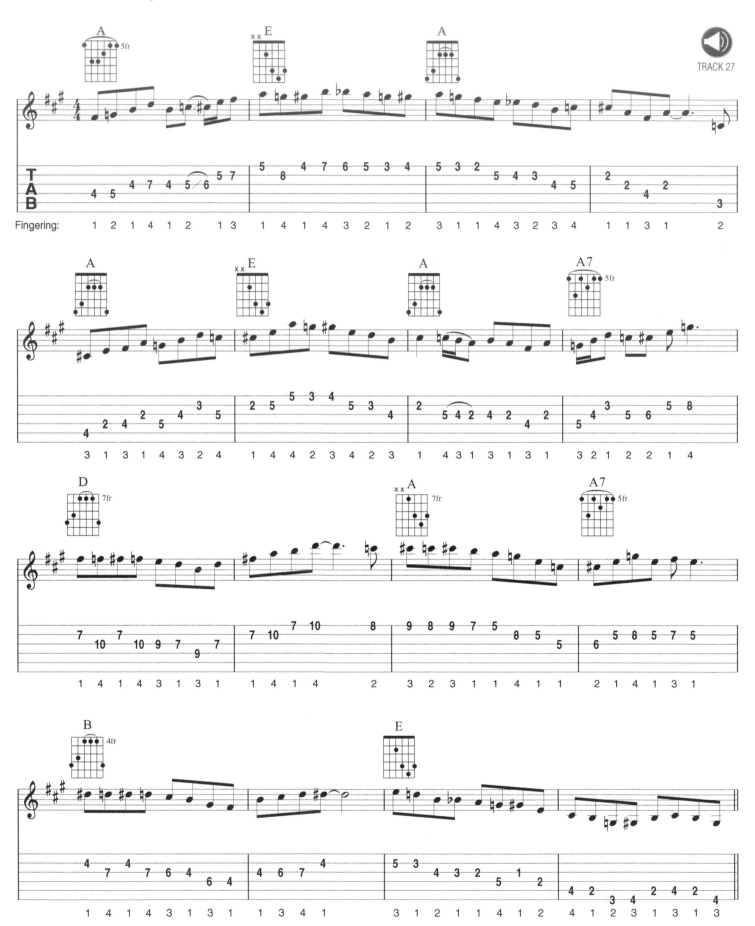

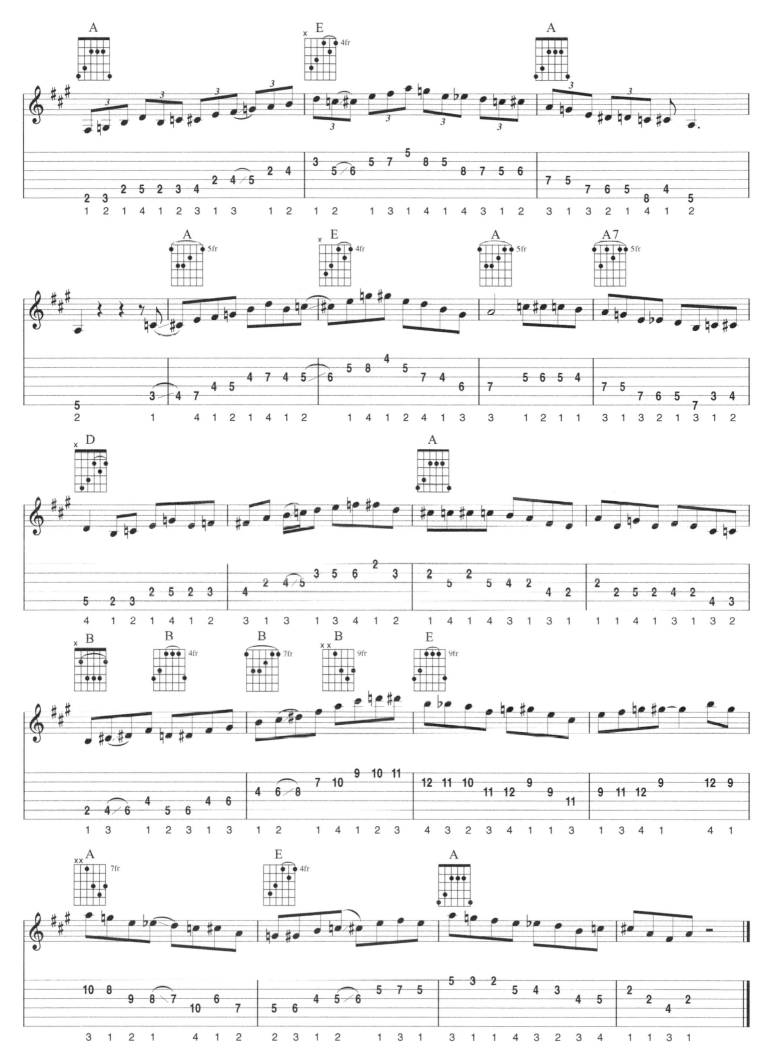

# Double Stops

## Simple Intervals

A *double stop* is two notes played simultaneously. The term is borrowed from violin technique, in which a pair of strings is "stopped" or sounded together at the same time. Double stops are an integral part of country guitar and are played with hybrid right-hand technique. To gain insight into how double stops are generated and applied, we must first understand intervals and the shapes they make on the fretboard.

An interval is defined as the distance between two notes. This distance has two characteristics: 1) number name, and 2) quality name. Below are the degrees of a C major scale. The distance from the tonic (C) and each subsequent note is measured with a number. The number increases as the distance gets larger, eventually reaching the octave. To determine the number of any interval, treat the lower note as "one" and count through the musical alphabet until reaching the desired note. C to G is a 5th, C to A is a 6th, etc.

The second characteristic of an interval is its quality. Quality makes the number names more specific. This example shows the intervals created by the notes of the C major scale in relation to the root, each labeled with its quality and number. In a major scale, intervals are either major or perfect.

If we lower major and perfect intervals by a half step, we generate the new intervals shown in the following example. These intervals share the same numbers as those in the major scale but have different qualities.

30

# Common Double-Stop Shapes

In country guitar, double stops are commonly used in intervals of 3rds, 4ths, 5ths, 6ths, and tritones. Below are several examples of how these shapes look on the fretboard. Notice that many of these interval shapes can be played on different pairs of strings, and all of them are movable anywhere on the neck. Play through these using your middle and ring fingers for those intervals that are on adjacent strings. Use your pick and middle finger, or pick and ring finger for those on non-adjacent strings. Left-hand fingering is not important. We are only trying to visualize and hear these different intervals.

## Intervals Within the Major Scale

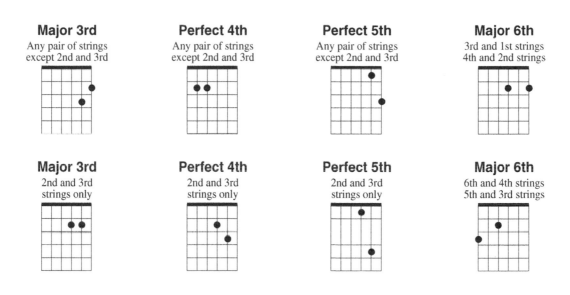

## Intervals Outside of the Major Scale

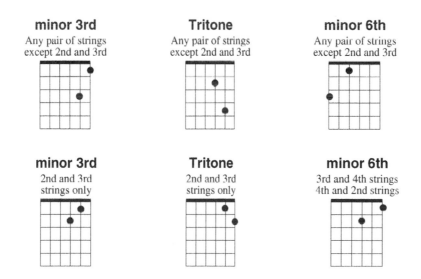

# Harmonizing the Major Scale with 6ths

Below is a G major scale harmonized in 6ths. The lower note begins on the 3rd (B) while the upper note starts on the tonic (G). We proceed stepwise up the neck on the third and first strings, making sure each double stop uses only notes from the G major scale (G–A–B–C–D–E–F#). Harmonization using only scale tones is called *diatonic*.

### G major, 3rd and 1st strings

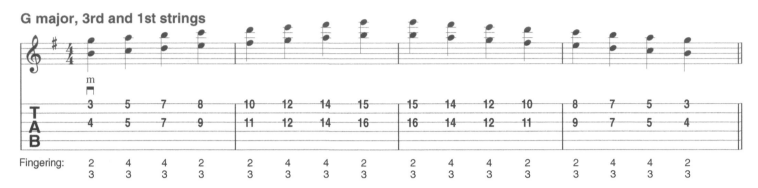

Once you are familiar with these shapes, move them to the fourth and second strings. The fingering is the same as for the G major scale, but because of the location of the first finger we are now in the key of C major. Follow the left-hand fingering, and use a combination of pick (⊓) and middle finger (m) on the right hand.

### C major, 4th and 2nd strings

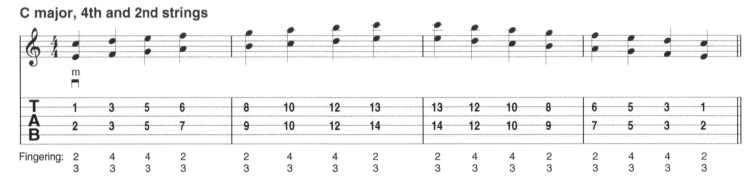

When playing 6ths in this fashion on the fifth and third strings, the fingerings are as shown. These fingerings remain the same on the sixth and fourth strings. The two harmonizations below are in the keys of A and E major, respectively.

### A major, 5th and 3rd strings

### E major, 6th and 4th strings

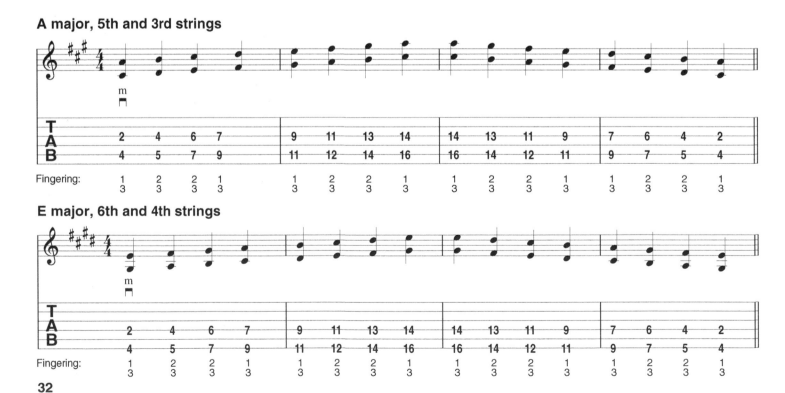

# Licks Using 6ths

Follow all left- and right-hand fingerings exactly as written, and practice these lines in all keys. The first lick is played over a D major chord. Note the chromaticism on beats 2 and 3 in measure 1.

TRACK 28

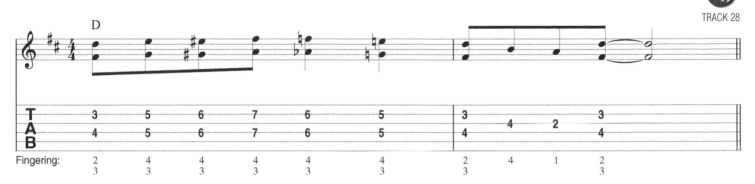

This is a great intro lick in G major. The second and third measures are played over the V chord before resolving to the I.

TRACK 29

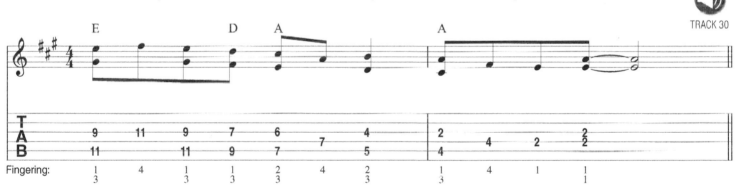

Here's a descending line in A. Note the use of both single notes and double stops.

TRACK 30

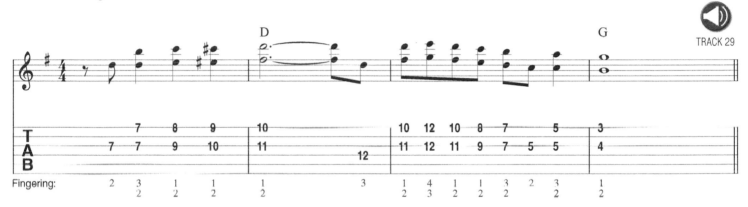

For this chicken pickin' lick in G, first alternate the pick on each triplet, then pluck hard on the E string so it slaps against the frets.

TRACK 31

33

## Harmonizing the Hexatonic Major Scale with 3rds and 4ths

Eliminating the major scale's 7th tone generates the "hexatonic major" scale. This six-note scale is shown below in A major. The scale is played up the neck on strings 3 and 2.

**A Hexatonic Major Scale**

By stacking every other note (root and 3rd, 2nd and 4th, 3rd and 5th, etc.) we produce the double stops shown below. These include two sets of intervals: 1) major and minor 3rds, and 2) perfect 4ths. With these intervals, we can create some very useful double-stop lines. Use your pick (⊓) and middle (m) finger on the double stops, or for more snap, try the middle (m) and ring (a) fingers together.

**A Hexatonic Major Scale Harmonized in 3rds and 4ths**

When soloing with double stops, it's important to use a variety of intervals. The hexatonic major scale is ideal for this because it contains both 3rds and 4ths.

## Licks Using the Hexatonic Major Scale

In the following examples play double stops with the middle and ring fingers. For single notes, use down-strokes with the pick.

This line is played over A, and is completely diatonic. Let the first double stop ring out while picking the F♯ on the fourth string.

TRACK 32

This example is also over A or A7. Note the use of chromatic passing tones. These give the line a much richer harmonic texture.

TRACK 33

Here is a descending line in C. Once again, many of the double stops are linked together with passing tones.

TRACK 33 (cont'd)

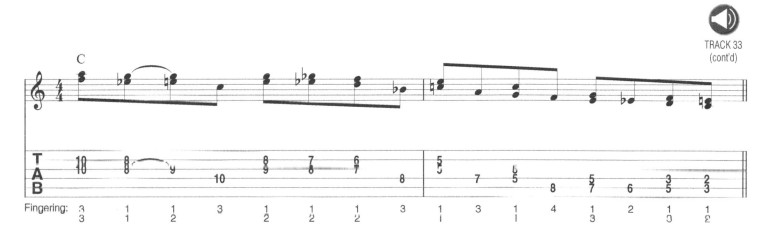

In this example, double stops are used to outline a chord change in the key of G major. The first bar is over the V (D7), then the lick resolves to I (G) in the second measure.

TRACK 34

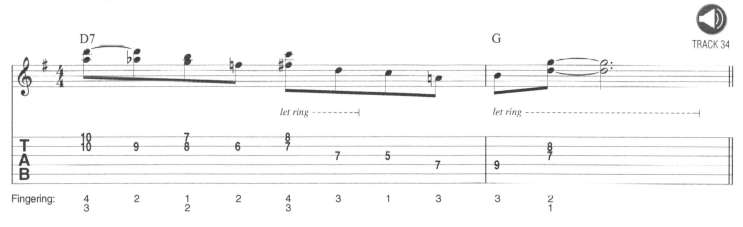

## Harmonizing Parallel Major and Minor Pentatonics with 4ths and Tritones

Another great way to generate double stops is to combine major and minor pentatonic scales. This is achieved by a parallel relationship. When scales share the same root but differ in quality they are said to be parallel. For example, the parallel minor of C major is C minor, and the parallel major of E minor is E major. This relationship is particularly effective when applied to pentatonic scales. Below are two pentatonic scales stacked on top of one another. The bottom tones start on the 3rd degree of A major pentatonic, while the top notes begin on the ♭7th degree of A minor pentatonic. The resulting harmony is a series of tritones and perfect 4ths.

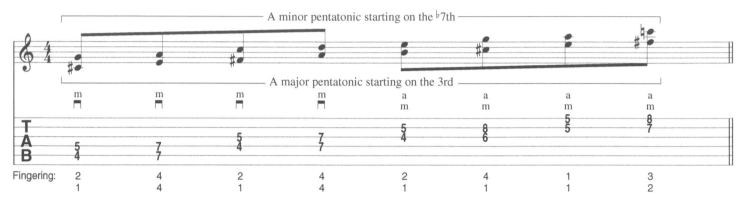

In this example, the lower notes begin on the 5th of A minor pentatonic and upper tones begin on the root of A major pentatonic. This yields intervals of perfect 4ths, major 3rds and minor 3rds. Follow all left- and right-hand fingerings carefully and play these examples descending as well. Make sure to practice them in all keys.

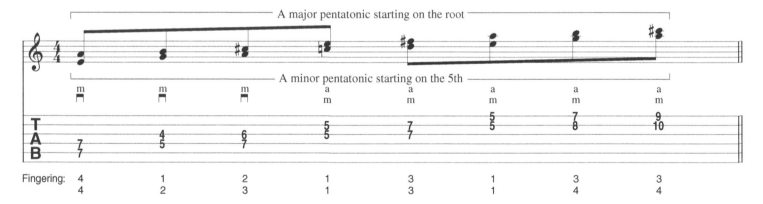

## Licks Using Parallel Major and Minor Pentatonics

Below are several double-stop lines created from stacking parallel major and minor pentatonic scales. Play these slowly and pay careful attention to all right- and left-hand fingerings. Once you've mastered these lines and feel comfortable playing them up to tempo, be sure to transpose them to different keys. The first three licks are over A, D, and E chords and can be practiced over any type of I–IV–V progression in A major, such as a 12-bar blues.

The first example is based in the fifth position around the A blues scale. The first double stop is bent by pushing both fingers up toward the sixth string.

TRACK 35

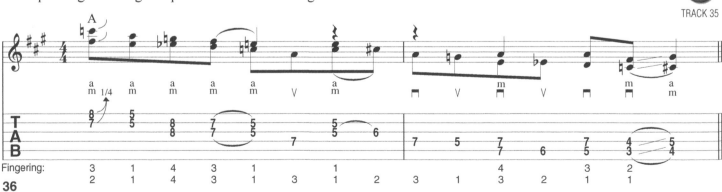

This lick works its way down in seventh position. Try to visualize the different D major chord shapes that surround the double stops. Let the higher tones sustain while playing the single notes underneath.

TRACK 36

Our next example works its way down from seventh to second position. Pay special attention to the way in which pull-offs and slides are used to smoothly link the double stops.

TRACK 37

This one begins in ninth position and ends on an open G chord. The first two double stops are played staccato, which means short and detached. For maximum twang, pull hard with your middle (m) and ring (a) fingers and let the high notes sustain while picking underneath.

TRACK 38

## Accuracy

String bending in country guitar differs from that found in blues and rock in two important ways: accuracy and oblique motion. Accuracy refers to the pitch and stability of the string being bent. Because many country licks involve bending in and out of chord tones it is critical that the string being stretched stay in tune. Oblique motion refers to the technique of playing one or more strings while a bent note is held in place. These bends must be properly intonated as well. To better develop precision and accuracy we will first examine unison bends. In the example below, the note on the third string is pushed up a whole step (two frets) by the third finger (reinforced by the second finger behind). Once the desired pitch is achieved, it is held in place and the same (unison) tone is played by the first finger on the second string. This process is repeated up the neck, outlining a D major pentatonic scale. Listen closely to the bent note and be sure it is identical to the pitch on the second string. Your first finger remains planted throughout, and your second finger is placed a fret below the third for support.

TRACK 39

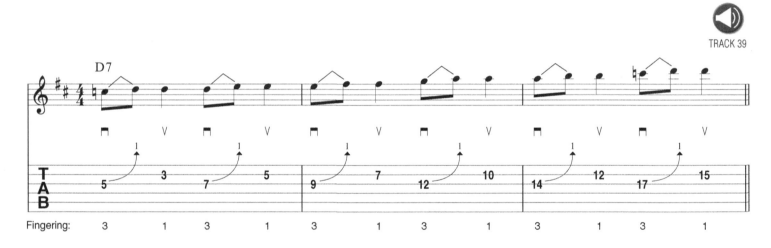

The process is repeated on the first and second strings with slightly different finger spacing. This example outlines a G major pentatonic scale.

TRACK 39
(cont'd)

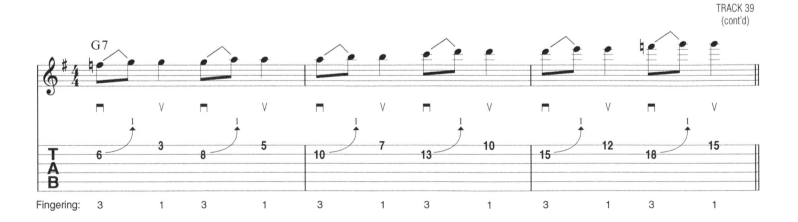

# Oblique Bends

The next two examples combine oblique motion with unison bends. The bent note is seen as a chord tone, in this case the 3rd, which is struck alternately while the melody is played on the next higher string. The bend is then released before resolving to the tonic in the second measure. Play the lower string with your pick and use the middle finger for the higher string. The left-hand fingering is the same as before.

Be sure to visualize the chord shapes that relate to these licks!

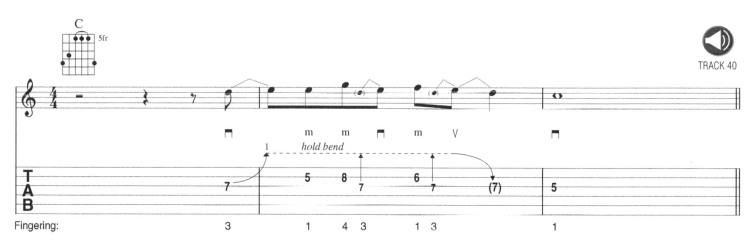

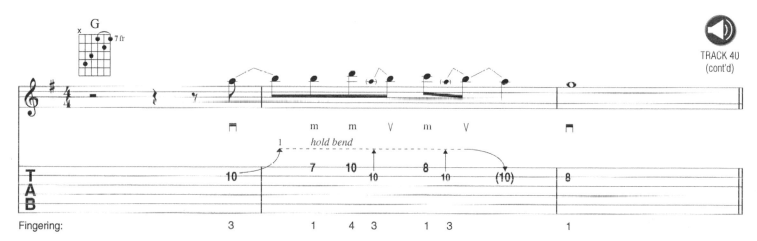

There are many ways to incorporate oblique motion into bends. The following demonstrate three of the most common. Once again, the chord shape that relates to each line is shown. It's a good idea to play these before and after each lick. The more ideas and licks you relate to a particular chord, the more you'll have to draw upon when soloing. In the second measure of each example, a single-note line is used to resolve the lick to its tonic. They are also shown over the I, IV, and V chords in the key of A major (A, D, and E). This will allow you to quickly assimilate these licks into a typical chord progression in A major like a 12-bar blues.

Here the ♭7th is bent up to the root. The line then resolves in fifth position.

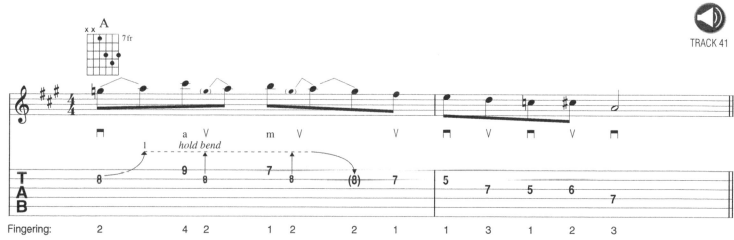

39

In this example, the 2nd is bent up to the major 3rd, a very common move in country. Note the use of a 6th in the second measure.

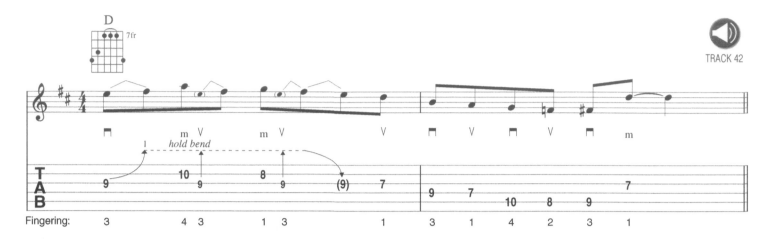

By raising the 4th to the 5th we create a very bluesy-sounding bend. This feel is continued in the second measure by descending down the E blues scale.

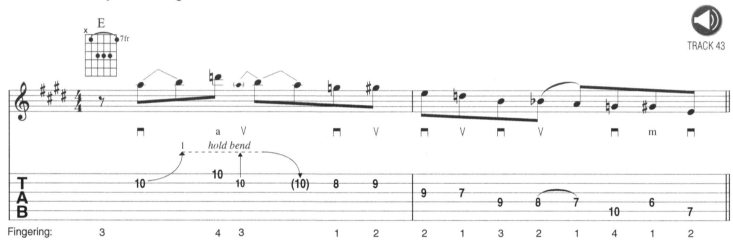

## Scale-Type Bending Licks

You can also play bends from the scales discussed in Chapter 2. The following examples demonstrate some cliché licks contained within the various pentatonic and composite scales. This line comes from the C blues scale.

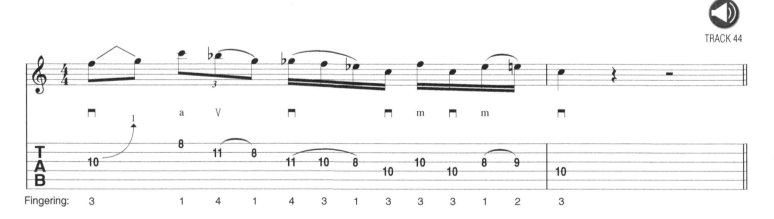

This lick combines bending with double stops, à la Chuck Berry.

TRACK 45

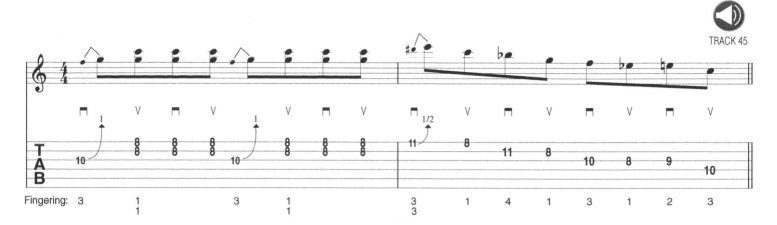

Here's a common move in F minor pentatonic. As the bend is released you move directly into a pull-off. Strive for a smooth, legato (flowing and connected) sound.

TRACK 46

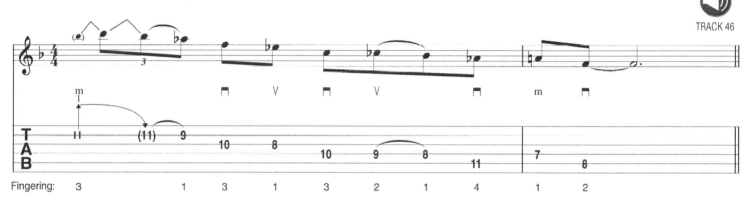

This line combines bending with right-hand muting. Gradually release the bend over the course of two measures while muting every other eighth note with the middle finger. Keep the mutes on the strong beats.

TRACK 47

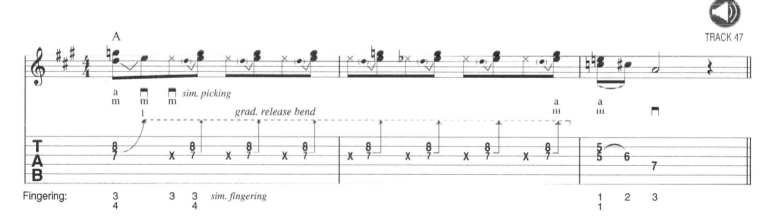

This unison bending lick from the G blues scale incorporates three open-string pull-offs.

TRACK 48

41

# Chord-Type Bending Licks

By bending one or both strings in a double stop, we can create some very interesting chord-type bends. These can be played on a static major, minor, or dominant seventh chord, or they can be linked together to create an entire progression. Like oblique bends, the following require that one, and in some cases two notes be held in place while another string is pushed up or pulled down. The overall effect is similar to a pedal steel guitar, where levers are used to raise notes a whole or half step.

In this common move the 2nd degree is bent to the 3rd while the root and 5th are held in place. This creates an A major chord.

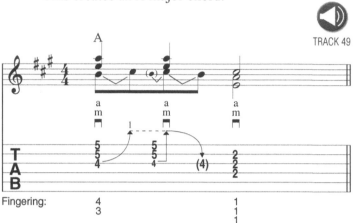

Here's a similar move on a different set of strings. This produces a D major chord.

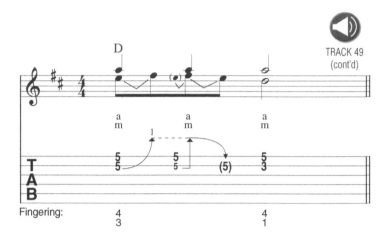

To play over E, the same idea is moved to a lower string set and finishes with a single-note line, punctuated by a double stop.

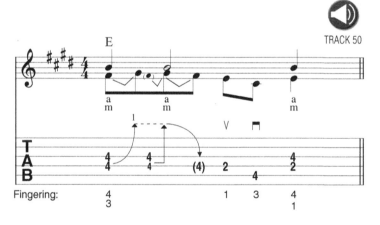

For this pedal steel lick in A, pull the bend down with your first finger while holding the lower tones in place.

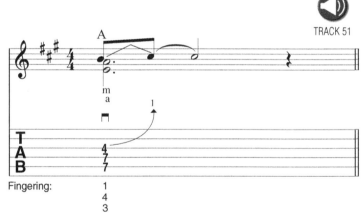

Here several chords are substituted over a D major tonality.

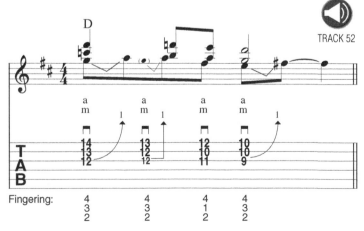

This lick over E7 utilizes a prebend, in which the string is bent before being picked.

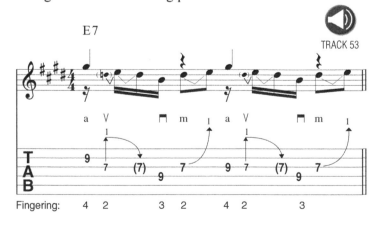

This pedal steel lick in A is punctuated with the 6th scale degree on the first string.

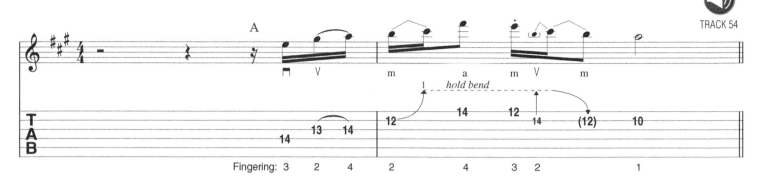

TRACK 54

Here's a repetitive lick using open strings. This is played over G and mimics the sound of a banjo.

TRACK 55

This is a good lick to play on minor chords. Both strings are pushed up simultaneously. Play this over E minor.

TRACK 56

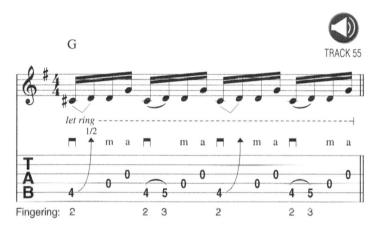

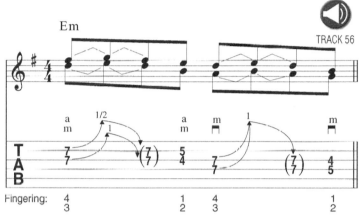

Here an entire chord sequence is played before resolving to A. Pull the bent notes down with your first finger.

TRACK 57

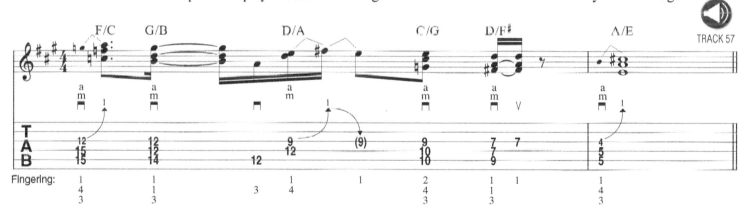

Another example of oblique motion, this lick moves between C and C7. Try resolving to F as well as to C in the second measure.

TRACK 58

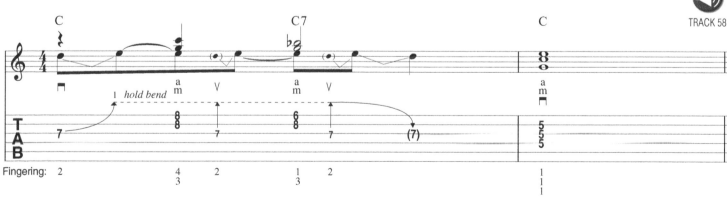

43

This is a similar oblique-motion lick on the lower strings. Try this with the G major pentatonic sliding scale.

TRACK 59

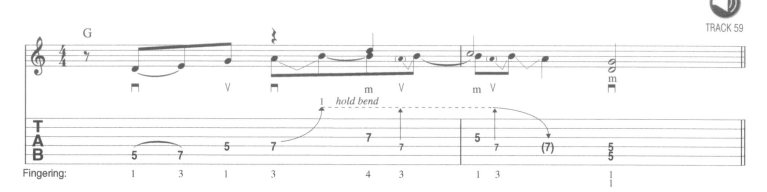

## Oblique Bends on Non-Adjacent Strings

Oblique motion does not always have to occur on adjacent strings. Some very interesting sounds can be achieved by skipping one or two strings. These bends commonly employ wider intervals, such as 6ths and 7ths.

This is a good intro lick in the key of B major. Let all notes ring out for their full values.

TRACK 60

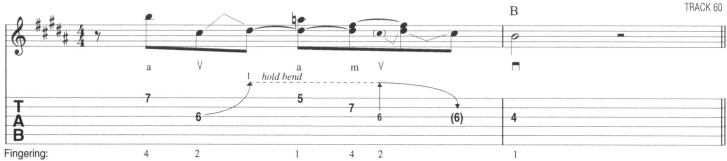

Here, the ♭7th is pulled up to the root before being punctuated with the octave. Play this lick over A.

TRACK 61

This is a similar idea over D. This time the root is punctuated with a 5th.

TRACK 61 (cont'd)

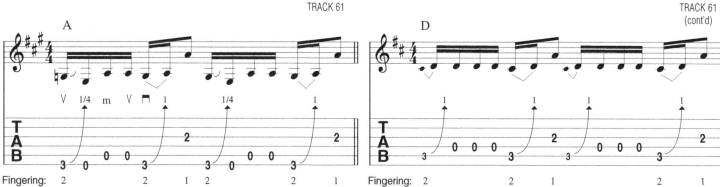

In this example major 6ths are moved chromatically by bending both strings simultaneously. Play this line over A or A7.

TRACK 62

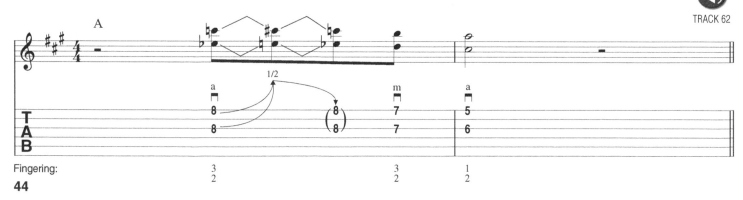

Here's the same idea on a different set of strings. Play on D or D7.

TRACK 62
(cont'd)

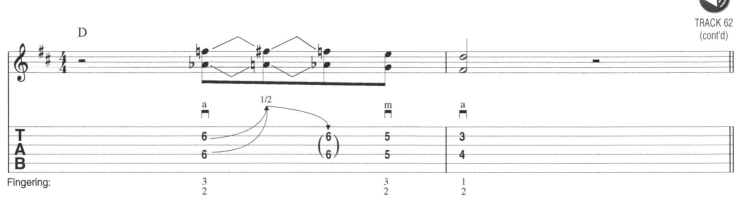

This line incorporates two new bends. The first has the root and ♭7th played against the 3rd of a C major chord. In the second measure, a half-step bend is used to end the single-note line.

TRACK 63

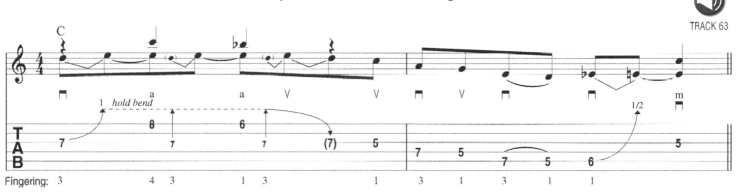

# Behind-the-Nut Bends

This technique involves depressing strings behind the nut with the left-hand fingers. These bends work best on Telecaster-style guitars because there's plenty of room between the strings and headstock to push down. All the following examples use both the first and second fingers to push down the designated string.

For this lick, plant your first and second fingers on the third string behind the nut. Play the top three strings, then push down, raising the third string by a half step. This creates an E major chord.

TRACK 64

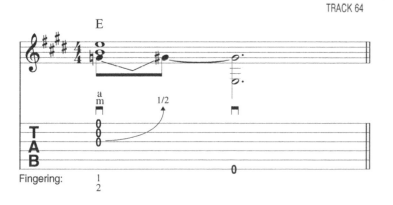

Here, the same string is bent, but this time a whole step. Use the same fingering for the bend and fret the C with your pinky. This outlines a D7 chord.

TRACK 65

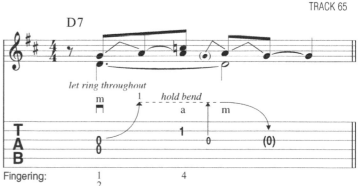

45

We can create a G major chord by pushing the fifth string down behind the nut to raise it a whole step and rolling the next two open strings. Use the same left-hand fingering behind the nut: the first and second fingers together.

TRACK 66

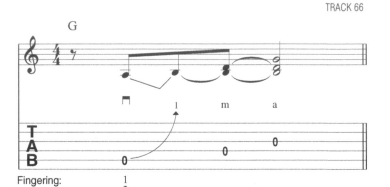

This line begins with a prebend. Start with the second string pushed up a half step. After releasing, plant the first and second fingers on the fourth string in preparation for the whole-step bend. This outlines a Cmaj7 chord and makes a good intro lick.

TRACK 67

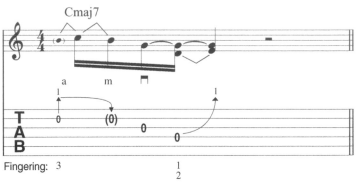

## Bends Gripping Two Strings

In this example, two bent strings move in opposite directions. This is called *contrary motion* because the pitches move away from one another. Pull the third string down a whole step with the first finger, and then catch the second string with the tip of the first finger. Release the third string back to pitch. This will cause the second string to raise a half step.

TRACK 68

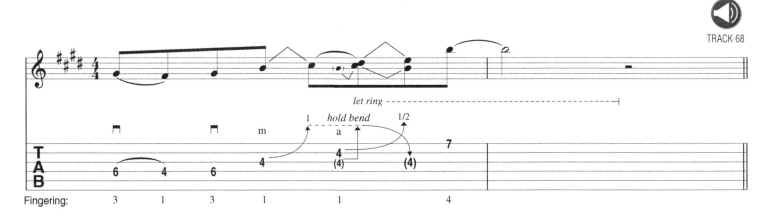

Here both strings move in the same direction, making it an example of *parallel motion*. This lick moves from D to A7, and back to D.

TRACK 69

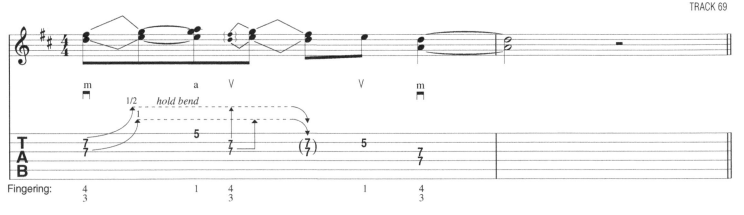

# Chord Progression for "Faux Steel"

Below is the chord progression for the solo, "Faux Steel." Roman numerals are used to track chord movement throughout the key, and simple open-string voicings are shown. Note the use of a secondary dominant chord (B) in measure 6. Also of interest is the tag in the last three measures. A *tag* is a harmonic or melodic device that punctuates the ending of a song.

## Sample Solo: "Faux Steel"

The following solo utilizes many bends discussed in this chapter and introduces a few new ideas as well. The chord forms these lines are based upon are shown above the staff. Try playing through the solo using only these shapes. This will help you visualize and block off the different areas of the fretboard being used. When you begin to learn the solo, follow all the left- and right-hand fingerings, and pay special attention to how the licks are joined together to achieve a cohesive sound.

TRACK 70

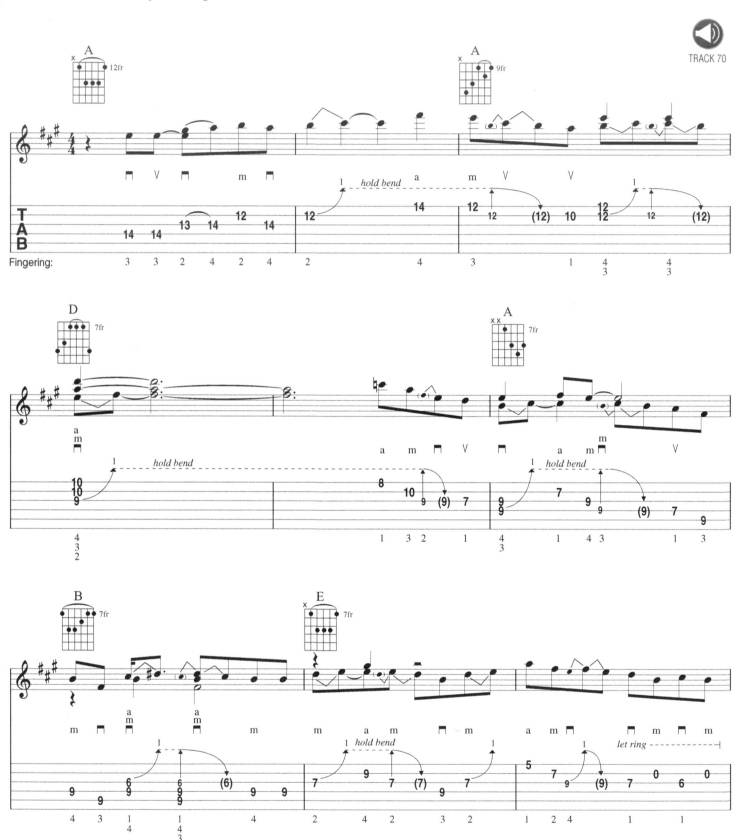

# Open-String Licks

The combination of fretted and open strings is an integral part of country guitar. This technique is applied in two ways: first as single-note scale-type lines, and secondly, in chord-like double-stop licks. When applied to scales, the alternation of fretted and open strings creates a cascading harp-like effect. With double stops, open strings are used to set up repetitive patterns and act as common tones between chord changes.

## The Mixolydian Mode

The seven-note diatonic scale being used in each of these examples is called the Mixolydian mode. This mode begins on the 5th degree of its respective major scale and contains all the same tones in the same order, but starting on a different note, so that the arrangement of half steps and whole steps is changed.

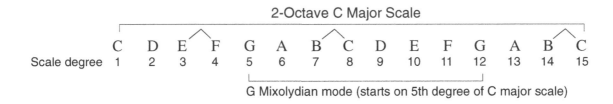

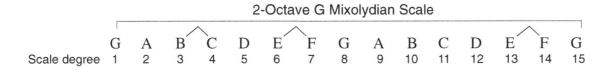

Notice that when analyzed from its root, the Mixolydian mode has the same construction as the major scale, with the exception of a minor 7th degree. While its primary application is over the V7 chord, the Mixolydian mode is also often used over a tonic (I) major triad instead of the major scale, or over a tonic (I7) dominant seventh chord. (Mixolydian should not be used over a Imaj7 chord, where the major scale is the best fit.)

Mixolydian is especially good for playing over the many dominant chords (1–3–5–$\flat$7) and major triads that abound in country music: I, IV, V, and secondary dominants, for example the B major triad in the key of A (V7/V or II7), as seen in "Faux Steel."

# Mixolydian Mode Using Open Strings

Because of the limited notes available as open strings, the keys of A, G, E, D, and C are best for using open-string licks. Below are five Mixolydian scale fingerings that work over the I major or I7 chord in each key. Play through these examples slowly and follow left- and right-hand fingerings closely. Let all open strings ring out as long as possible!

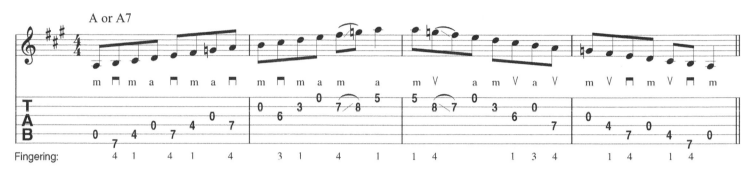

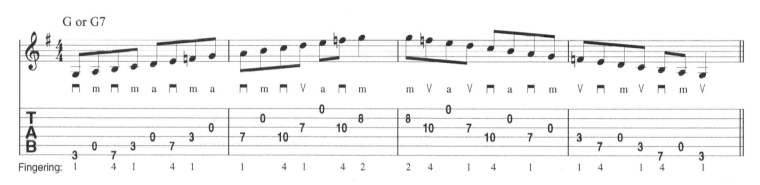

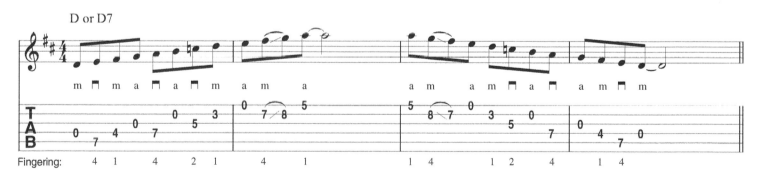

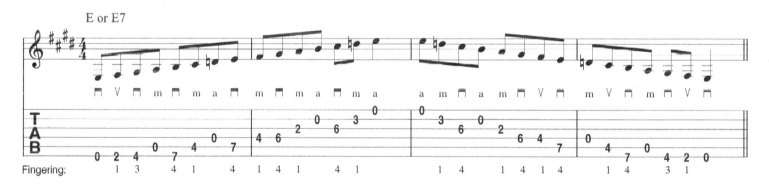

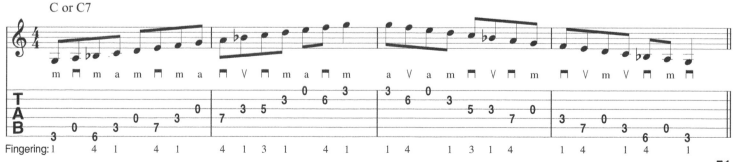

# Open-String Scale Licks

Once you're comfortable with open-string Mixolydian scale fingerings, try incorporating some chromatic passing tones. The following licks utilize this idea. Notice the prevalence of major and minor seconds between open and fretted notes. This colorful clash of dissonance is a big part of both modern country and bluegrass guitar.

This descending line in G occurs entirely in seventh position and ends with an open-string double stop.

TRACK 71

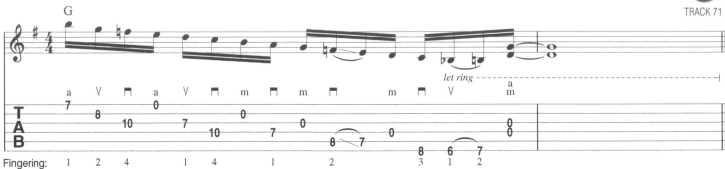

This bluesy lick in D descends through first position.

TRACK 72

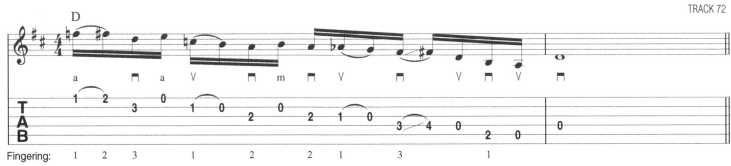

Open strings are ideal when switching positions on the neck. This example descends in A and moves from the fifth to the second position.

TRACK 73

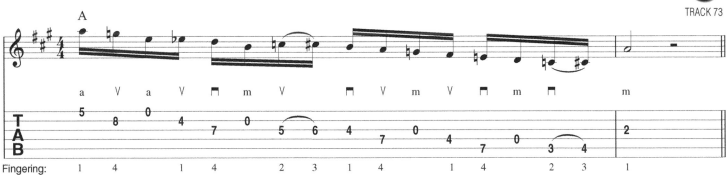

This lick moves down from the fifth to the third position and ends on a C major chord.

TRACK 73
(cont'd)

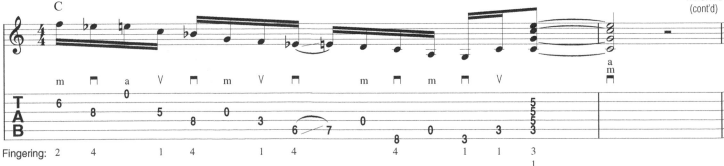

In this example, the line descends while the fingering moves up the neck. The lick ends with an E6/9 chord. Note the two-barre fingering for this chord.

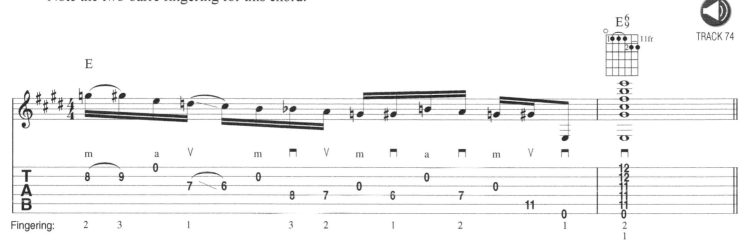

Here are some ascending open-string lines over the same five chord forms.

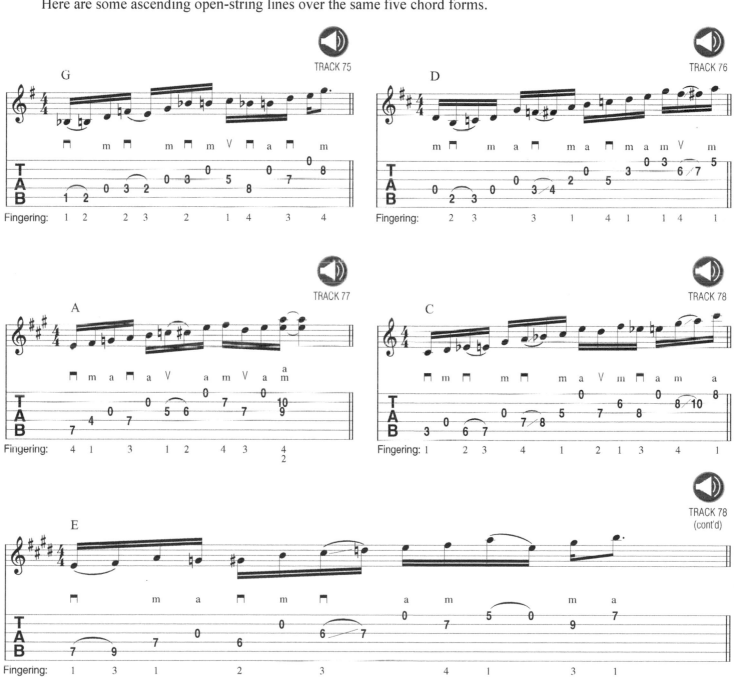

# Double Stops with Open Strings

The following double-stop line descends on the third and fourth strings and is played over a D major chord. Pluck with the middle and ring fingers throughout. Follow all left-hand slides and slurs (hammer-ons and pull-offs).

TRACK 79

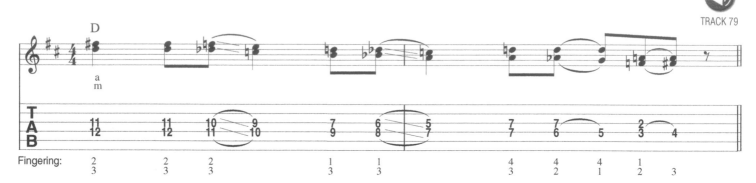

By thinking of the open D string as a chord tone (in this case the root), we can insert it after every eighth note in the above example. This generates the lick shown below. At faster tempos, this process gives double-stop lines more rhythmic momentum. Notice that each open D is played with an upstroke.

TRACK 79 (cont'd)

Here's a similar idea over a G major chord. In this example the open G string functions as the root.

TRACK 80

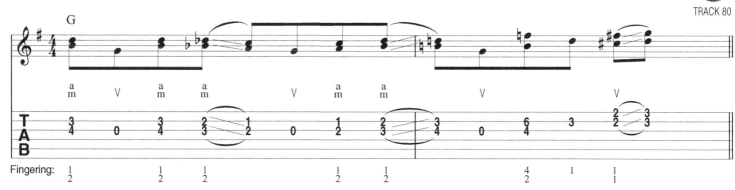

This ascending line in E major utilizes the open B string. B is the fifth of an E major chord.

TRACK 81

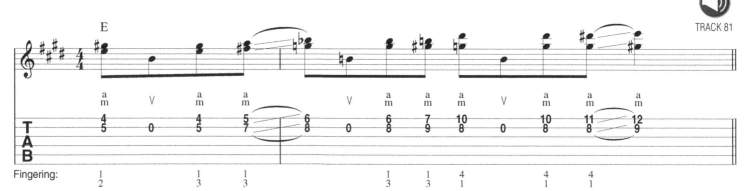

In this example, the open G acts as the 5th of a C major chord.

TRACK 82

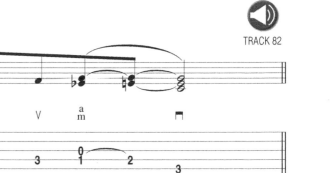

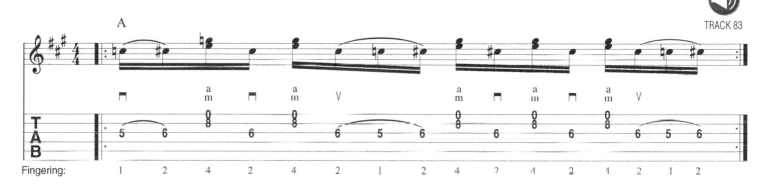

# Repetitive Patterns

During the course of a solo it is quite common to use short one- or two-measure licks that repeat and outline the chord being played. When applied to double stops this process often utilizes one or more open strings and is most effective at fast tempos. The following examples demonstrate this technique over the I, IV, and V chords in A (A, D7, and E7, respectively). Notice that each lick uses the open E string. This is the harmonic glue that holds all three lines together. Over A, E functions as the 5th.

TRACK 83

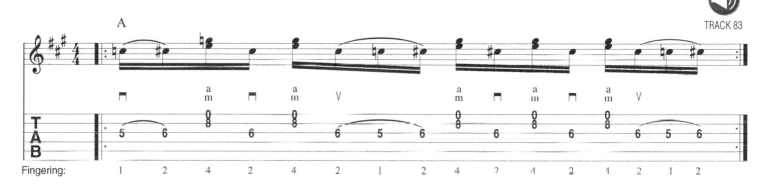

E can be thought of as the 9th of D7.

TRACK 84

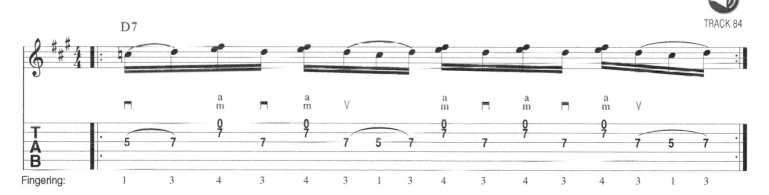

Over E7, E functions as the root.

TRACK 84 (cont'd)

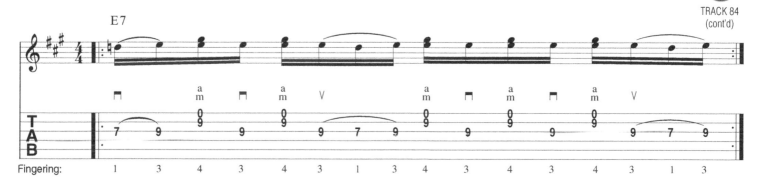

Hold down the fourth finger throughout each of the above examples.

# The Common Tone Concept Applied to Open-String Licks

Compare the notes in the following two fingerings:

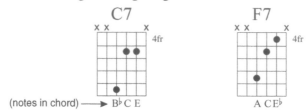

Notice that there is one note, in this case C, that is common to both chords. C is the root of the I chord and the 5th of the IV chord. When playing repetitive double stops over a I–IV progression, use of this common tone promotes smooth voice leading and accurately tracks the chord progression. The following example demonstrates the common tone concept over a I–IV progression in the key of C (C7–F7).

TRACK 85

Here is a similar idea over a I–IV change in A major. The fingering is identical to the previous example, but we've moved down three frets.

TRACK 85
(cont'd)

# Licks in the Styles of the Masters

In this chapter we will examine the styles of country music's most influential guitarists. Although an entire book could be written on this subject alone, I've kept the list rather short. Instead we will focus on each player's characteristics and techniques as they relate to the material in this book. Each of these players has had an enormous impact on my playing and development as a musician. It would be impossible to sum up their contribution in a few short examples! Therefore, the licks in this chapter should be viewed as short synopses of each style, rather than as verbatim transcriptions.

## Danny Gatton

Originally from Washington, D.C., Danny Gatton was well versed in country, rockabilly, jazz, and blues. His enormous talent and vast knowledge of different guitar styles lent to an "everything but the kitchen sink" attitude when soloing. The first example shows his approach to double stops. This repetitive figure in E major is played entirely with the flatpick and left-hand slurs. Practice this lick slowly and don't rush the sixteenth-note triplets (hammer-on, pull-off).

TRACK 86

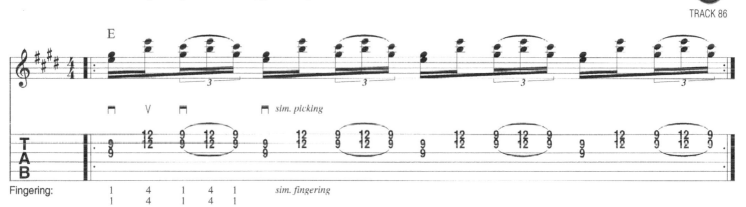

This single-note line in G comes out of a fingering Danny utilized for dominant seventh chords. Notice the absence of the root throughout. Omitting the tonic and starting on the 5th achieves a much more sophisticated sound. The various arpeggios produced by this line are shown in parentheses.

TRACK 87

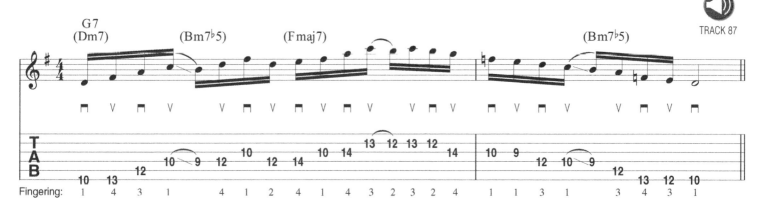

## Pete Anderson

Pete has been the guitarist and producer for Dwight Yoakam since the singer's first release in the early 1980s. Originally from Detroit, Michigan, Pete's style is heavily rooted in the blues. His stripped-down "less is more" approach distinguishes him from the multitude of hot Nashville pickers. The following shows how Pete emulates the sound of a pedal steel. Barre across the seventh fret with the first finger and let all notes ring out.

TRACK 88

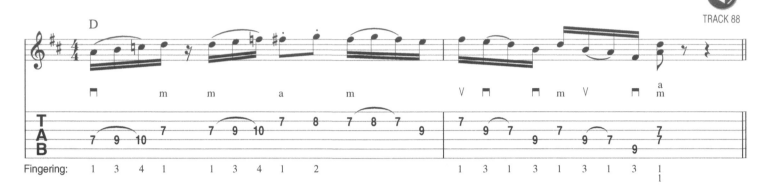

Here's a typical idea Anderson might play in the open E blues scale. Note the slight double-stop bend at the end of the first measure.

TRACK 89

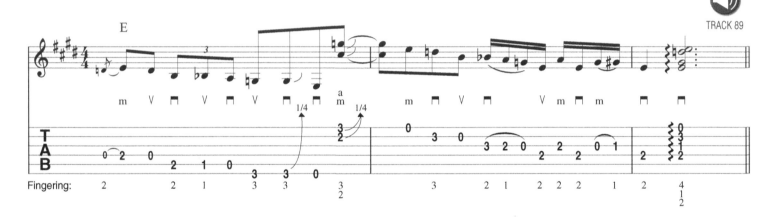

## Albert Lee

One of the most influential guitarists in the last thirty years, Englishman Albert Lee has certainly left his mark on country guitar! As a member of Emmylou Harris's Hot Band, Albert's amazing single-note runs and rapid-fire double stops were an integral part of the singer's earlier releases. A much sought-after side-man and session musician, Lee has worked with a wide range of artists including Eric Clapton, Ricky Skaggs, Rosanne Cash, Steve Morse, the Everly Brothers, Joe Cocker, and countless others.

The following lick demonstrates Albert's approach to chicken pickin'. Each muted triplet figure is played by partially fretting the note with the first, second, or third finger. This is followed by yanking the first string with the right-hand ring finger. The second measure contains a quick bend and descending double-stop figure. Albert's timing is impeccable, so make sure to practice this lick slowly before attempting it up to tempo.

TRACK 90

This example shows Albert's approach to single-note lines. The left-hand muting gives the line an interesting syncopated feel. Note the half-step bend in measure 1 and the areas where position shifts occur.

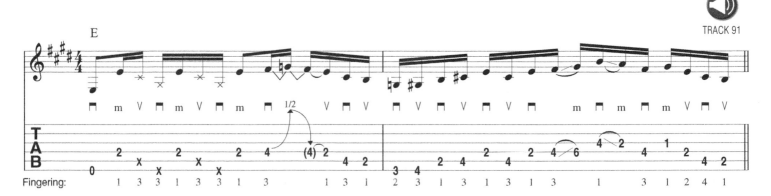

# Reggie Young

One of Nashville's "A" list session guitarists, Reggie has been part of the country and R&B scene for over forty years. Before moving to Nashville, Young was a member of the legendary Muscle Shoals studio team and an integral part of the "Memphis" R&B sound. His slick chord fills can be heard on countless recordings by Johnny Cash, Elvis Presley, Travis Tritt, Rodney Crowell, and hundreds of other top artists. The following two examples show Reggie's approach to double-stop fills. These lines can be seen as a C major pentatonic scale harmonized in 4ths and 5ths.

TRACK 92

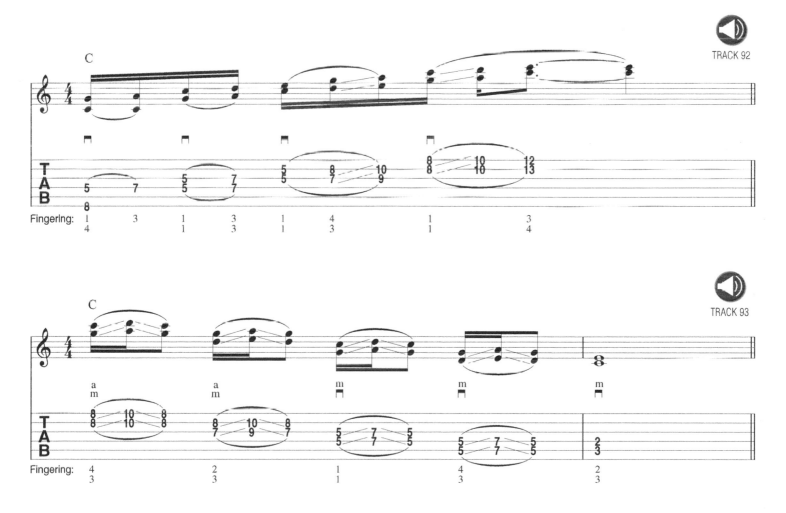

TRACK 93

# Ray Flacke

Like Albert Lee, Ray Flacke is originally from England. His cliché-free approach to rhythm and lead work has led to extended stints with such artists as Ricky Skaggs and Marty Stuart. After moving to Nashville in 1978 he entrenched himself in the city's competitive studio scene, recording with artists such as Patty Loveless, Emmylou Harris, Travis Tritt, Kathy Mattea, and countless others. The following demonstrates Ray's unique approach to double stops. This example involves muting with the right-hand middle finger while simultaneously picking a downstroke. This is followed by plucking the double stop with middle and ring fingers and sliding the shape up one fret. This process is repeated throughout the line.

TRACK 94

TRACK 95

# Brent Mason

It would be impossible to discuss the current state of country guitar without mentioning Brent Mason. For nearly two decades he's been on top of Nashville's active studio scene. His playing has contributed to hits by today's biggest artists, most notably Alan Jackson and George Strait. His recordings with fellow "Nashville Cat" Mark O'Connor, and his solo effort, *Hot Wired*, are incredibly creative and inspiring. Brent's style comes in part from the Albert Lee school of playing. His use of a thumbpick and penchant for syncopated rhythms along with funky double stops and burning single-note lines have helped redefine modern country guitar. The example below demonstrates Brent's approach to a repetitive lick in A. Strive for a fast, staccato sound.

TRACK 96

This line in E major begins with single-note triplets and finishes with open-string double stops. Notice the double-stop pull-offs in the last measure.

TRACK 97

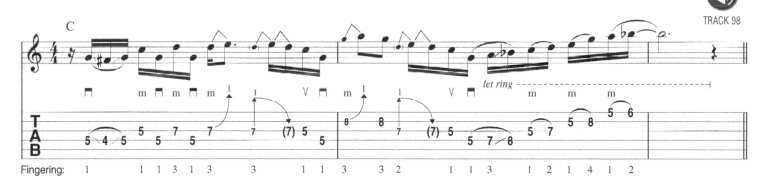

# Johnny Hiland

Johnny Hiland is a true phenomenon. The story of his rise to international recognition is almost as incredible as his playing. Disillusioned with college in his home state of Maine, Johnny headed to Nashville with little more than pocket change and his guitar. He quickly cultivated a name for himself and became lead guitarist with the prestigious Don Kelly Band. Displaying jaw-dropping technique and playing nonstop sets at Bob's Western World created a major industry buzz. He currently travels the world, playing festivals and conducting clinics. His debut album is available on Favored Nations.

The following example demonstrates Johnny's approach to pedal steel sounds. The bends on the third string are accomplished by pulling down, then releasing back to pitch. The bend on the second string is played normally. Strive for a rich legato sound.

TRACK 98

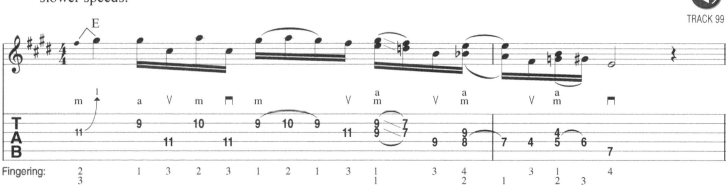

This lick in E major is based around a unison bend in measure 1, followed by a series of descending double stops. Johnny often plays this idea in songs with fast tempos, but it functions equally well at slower speeds.

TRACK 99

# Practice! Practice! Practice!

Practice, in large part, is devoted to learning and storing a wealth of information. This is dependent on two factors: the ability to play licks, chords, scales etc., in any key, and applying this information to practical situations (i.e. playing in bands, recording, or composing). This chapter outlines a systematic approach to practicing the material in this book.

## The Cycle of Fifths/Fourths

Major and minor scales (keys) can be built from each note of the chromatic scale. These twelve major and minor keys can be arranged in a circle like the face of a clock. Moving clockwise around the circle, each new key is a perfect 5th above the last. Moving counterclockwise, each key is a perfect 4th above the last. Each letter represents a different tonal center or key. Major keys are shown on the outside of the circle, while their relative minors are shown on the inside.

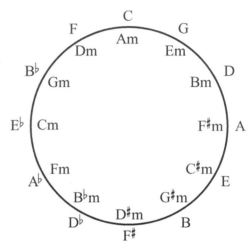

## Using the Cycle to Determine Keys

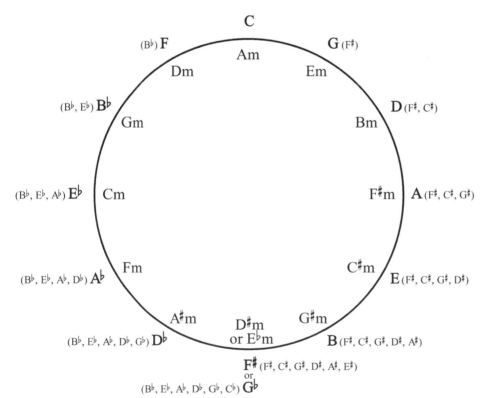

From the cycle, we can derive the key signature (sharps or flats) and the correct spelling for every major scale. Moving clockwise from C, one sharp (♯) is added to create each new scale. The previous sharp(s) are preserved, and the new sharp (♯) added is a perfect 5th higher. This process continues until reaching the key of F♯ major, which contains six sharps. Moving counterclockwise from C, one flat is added to create each successive new major scale. The previous flat(s) are preserved and the new flat is a perfect 4th higher than the previous one. This process continues until reaching the key of G♭, which contains six flats.

# Using the Cycle to Track Chord Progressions

The cycle of fifths is also useful for tracking chord progressions. Recall that the primary chords for any key are I, IV, and V, and the roots of these are easily seen in the cycle. The secondary dominant, V/V can also be visualized.

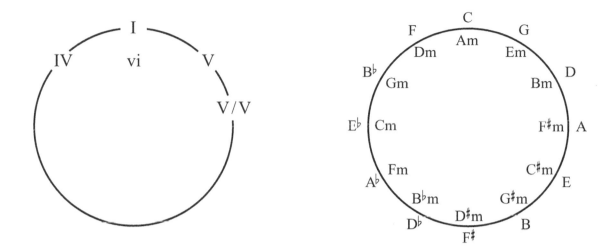

From the cycle, we can determine that C major contains the following primary chords: C, F, G or G7, and Am. The secondary dominant is D or D7. This process can be repeated anywhere in the cycle by following the above pattern. For example, B♭ major contains these primary chords: B♭, E♭, F or F7, and Gm. Its secondary dominant is C or C7. The diagrams below map the primary and secondary dominant chords in the two most common areas, with the root of the I chord on the sixth and fifth strings. Memorizing these fretboard "roadmaps" will enable you to play most country songs!

**Key of A Major**

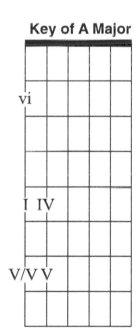

**Key of D Major**

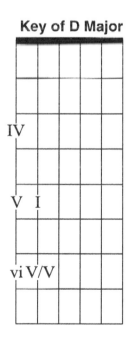

# Using the Cycle to Practice

As you can see, the cycle of fifths is an excellent way of learning keys, mapping chord progressions, and visualizing the fretboard. It's also a great tool for practicing and incorporating new licks into your musical vocabulary. The following eight-step procedure outlines how this is done.

1. Learn the lick in the position and key in which it is written.

2. Determine which of the five chord shapes (C, A, G, E, D) best fits the lick.

3. Using the chord shape as a guide, play the lick clockwise through the cycle.

4. For each key, play the corresponding chord before and after the lick.

5. Relearn the lick in a different position and string grouping. Determine which chord shape best fits.

6. Move this new fingering around the cycle, playing the chord before and after the lick.

7. Play the lick around the cycle, alternating between the two different positions and chord forms.

8. Incorporate the lick into your playing by practicing it through a common I–IV–V progression.

The following example illustrates this process by using an oblique string-bending lick from Chapter 6.

# Practicing Licks Around the Cycle

**Step 1**. Learn the lick in the original key.                    **Step 2**. Determine the chord shape.

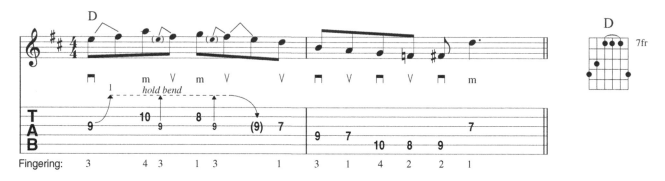

**Step 3**. Use the chord shape as a guide and play the lick clockwise through the cycle of fifths.

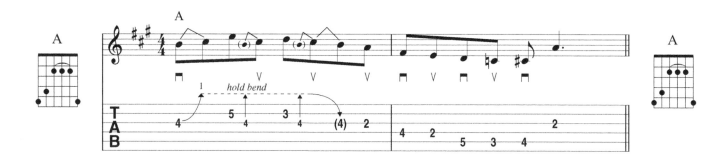

**Step 4**. Play the chord before and after each lick.

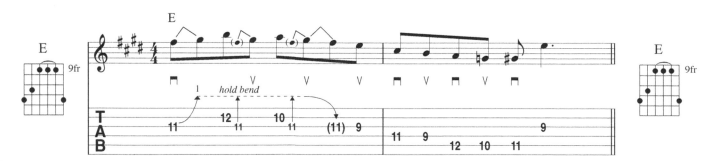

Continue around the cycle until the original key, D, is reached.

**Step 5**. Relearn the lick in a new position and string grouping. Determine which chord shape fits.

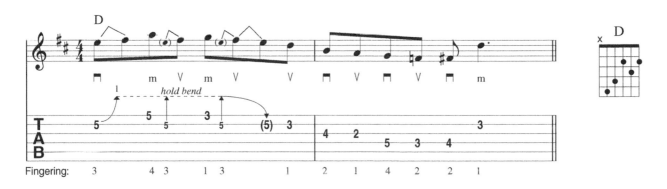

**Step 6**. Play the new fingering around the cycle.

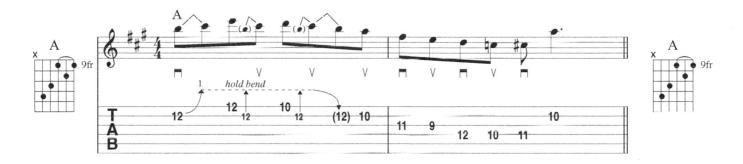

*Play the chord before and after each lick.*

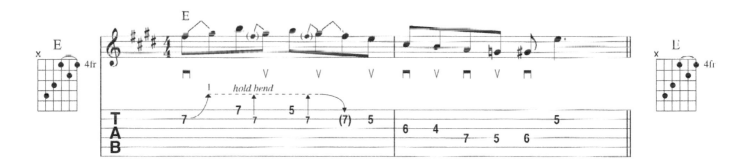

Continue around the cycle until reaching the original key of D.

**Step 7**. Play the lick around the cycle, alternating between the two different positions and chord forms.

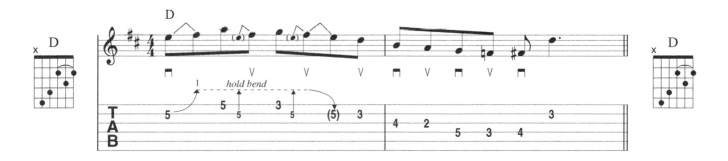

Continue around the cycle until the original key, D, is reached.

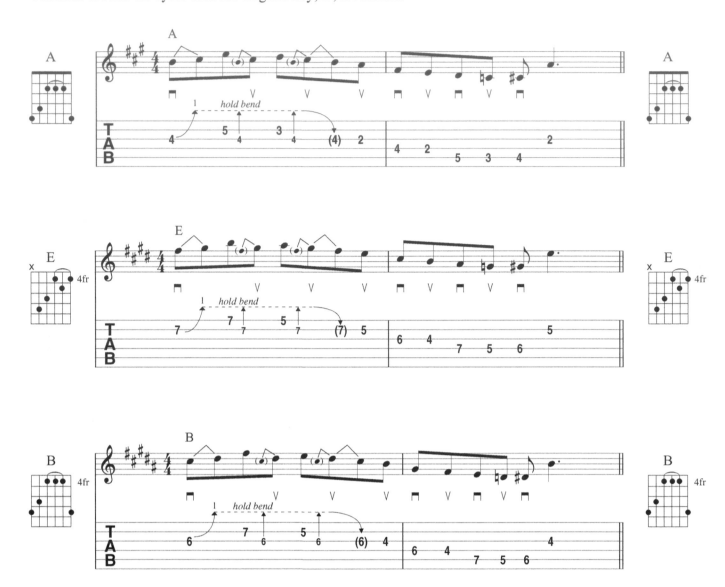

**Step 8**. Incorporate the lick into your playing by practicing it through a simple I, IV, V progression.

First, pick a key, then map out the chord shapes to be used. Here is the progression in E major.

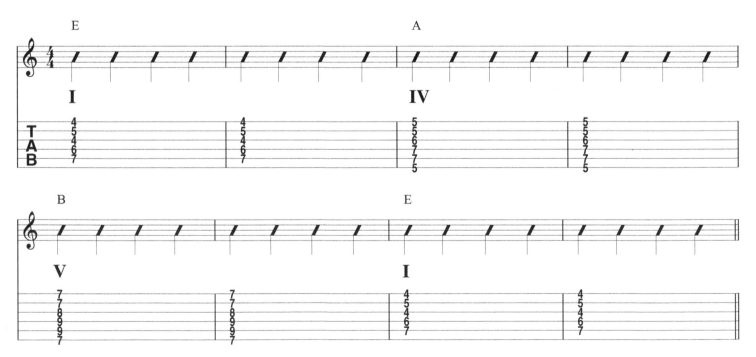

Next, insert the licks into the previous progression. Use the chord shapes as a visual guide. Repeat this two-stage process in every key!

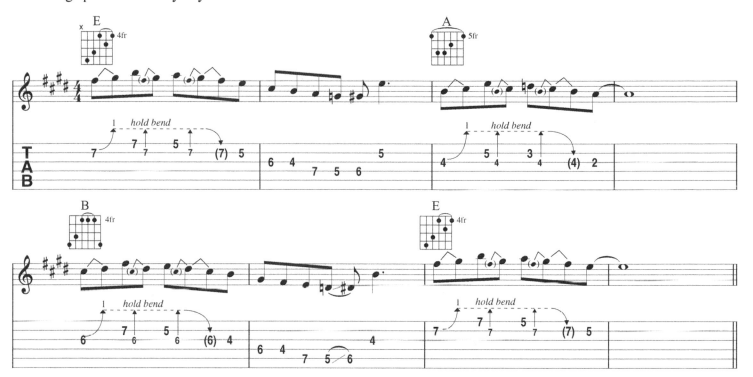

## Practice Tools

### Metronome

The most common tool used when practicing is the metronome. This device keeps your playing rhythmically accurate by keeping time with audible clicks. The clicks are measured in beats per minute, and the tempo (speed) can be adjusted from very slow to extremely fast. Set the metronome to click the beats corresponding to the bottom number of the time signature. For example, when playing in time signatures with the number 4 on the bottom, set the metronome to click in quarter notes. Smaller note values within the meter, such as eighth notes, sixteenth notes, and triplets are subdivided between the clicks. When practicing with a metronome, find a comfortable starting tempo and slowly increase the speed until the desired tempo is reached.

### Drum Machine

Drum machines are similar to a metronome but produce several different note values simultaneously. For example, a typical unit can play eighth notes on the hi-hat, quarter notes on the bass drum, and accent counts 2 and 4 on the snare drum, producing a backbeat common in most popular music. Like a metronome, the tempo can be adjusted.

### Backing Tracks

Backing tracks are recordings that contain bass, drums, and a harmonic instrument such as keyboards or guitar. They are available in many different styles and include a chart of the different chord progressions used. These are very helpful when exploring the sounds of different scales and licks. Although the tempos are fixed, they often include slow, moderate, and fast tempo songs.

### Recordings

Playing with recordings of your favorite artist is a great way to develop your ear. There are several ways to practice this. First, determine the key and strum the chords along with the song. Once the key and chord progression are established, you can practice various rhythm guitar techniques and fills. Second, find points of interest and determine what technique is being used, e.g. bends, double stops, chicken pickin', or open-string licks. These can then be transcribed loosely or note-for-note.

# Equipment

This chapter is meant as a guide to help you better understand what goes into achieving a good country guitar tone. This is a very subjective topic, and ultimately, decisions regarding equipment and settings should be made by you, the player. Keep in mind that trial and error play an important role in developing your own distinctive sound. Don't be afraid to experiment!

## Guitars

There are four main factors to consider when selecting a guitar: neck, body, pickups, and bridge assembly.

### Neck

Country guitarists generally prefer thin necks, like those associated with Fender-style guitars such as Telecasters or Stratocasters. These allow for greater control and ease of playing when executing the various techniques discussed in this book. Fretboards are typically either maple or rosewood. Maple boards have a coating of polyurethane or lacquer and are brighter in sound. Rosewood boards have no finish and often have a much smaller fretboard radius (curve) than their maple counterparts.

### Body

When selecting a body style for a country tone, avoid semi-hollowbody and archtop guitars, as their large cavities promote feedback.

Solidbody guitars are constructed of a variety of hardwoods, such as mahogany, ash, alder, and walnut. Denser woods, such as mahogany, increase natural sustain, but are very heavy. A popular option is to have a maple top laminated to a lighter wood, such as ash or alder. Solidbodies contain one or two cutaways (horns). The bottom cutaway is the most important as it allows access to the higher frets.

When shopping for a guitar, play it unamplified with the body pressed against you. With a good instrument, you should feel and hear the sustain without an amplifier.

### Pickups

Pickups are either single- or double-coil (humbucker) in design and can be used independently or together. Standard Telecaster guitars use two single-coil pickups, one installed at an angle in the bridge plate and the other positioned up toward the neck. A three-way switch allows you to select either pickup or a blend of the two. Although rather thin and trebly, the use of the bridge pickup on a Telecaster is the "industry standard" for today's country guitar sound. Stratocasters contain three single-coil pickups located at the bridge, middle, and neck. Most Strats contain a five-way switch allowing for numerous pickup combinations and a greater variety of tones. Double-coil humbucker pickups are associated with Les Paul-style guitars. These have a much richer and bassier sound than their single-coil counterparts.

### Bridge Assembly

There are two different types of bridge assembly on solidbody electrics: fixed and tremolo. Tremolo units can be depressed, and in some cases raised, by the use of springs and a metal arm (whammy bar). Because tremolos can interfere with the intonation of multiple-string bends, most country guitarists prefer fixed bridges, like those found on Telecasters.

# Strings

In order to play many of the examples in this book, a set of extra light to light gauge strings should be used. .009 – .042 gauge strings are recommended. A better tone can be achieved with .010 – .046 gauge strings, but they are much harder on the hands in terms of bending and right-hand technique.

# Amps

There are three categories to consider when selecting an amplifier: solid-state (transistor), tube (valve), and hybrid (combination).

Solid-state amplifiers are very dependable and affordable. However, transistor circuitry can cause a harsh and brittle tone, especially at higher volumes. This is due to the uneven harmonics produced.

Tube amplifiers produce very even harmonics and generate a rich, warm sound. These amps are more expensive and require the replacement of vacuum tubes and periodic maintenance. Despite this, most professionals prefer tube amps when recording or performing.

Hybrid amps are often a good compromise between solid-state and tube amps. These have an all-tube pre-amp stage followed by a solid-state power stage.

# Effect Pedals

A country guitarist should have and be familiar with one or all of the following devices: electronic tuner, volume pedal, delay (echo device), distortion, and compressor.

## Volume Pedals

Volume pedals can be used in three ways:

Inserted between guitar and amp allows foot control of the signal being sent from the guitar to the amp.

Inserted after your guitar and electronic tuner allows you to tune without being heard through the amplifier. Your guitar volume remains ON while the volume pedal is OFF.

Inserted before the delay provides a rich volume "swell." This is most effective when imitating pedal-steel sounds.

## Delays

Delay is an echo device that provides anything from a quick slap-back effect to a long-repeated echo. Older delay units were analog or tape fed. Today's units are digital and contain three main settings: delay time, feedback (repeats), and effect level.

Delay time adjusts the speed of the echo, typically from 30 milliseconds to 1 second intervals.

Feedback controls the number of repeats, from one repeat to, in some cases, infinite repeats.

Effects level controls the overall volume of the echo.

The following exemplify three common delay settings:

**Slap Back** is an extremely fast repeat associated with rockabilly and often used in place of reverb.

Settings
Delay Time:           ±100 milliseconds
Feedback (Repeat):    Off (1 repeat)
Effects Level:        Slightly lower than *initial signal

**Medium Delay** works well for filling out chordal and/or arpeggiated riffs.

Settings
Delay Time:           ±200 milliseconds
Feedback (Repeat):    3 to 5 repeats
Effects Level:        Slightly lower than *initial signal

**Long Delay** works well for rich swells and pedal-steel sounds.

Settings
Delay time:           800 milliseconds
Feedback (Repeat):    2 to 3 repeats
Effects Level:        1/2 to 1/3 *initial signal

*Initial signal refers to the volume your guitar produces with the delay pedal OFF.

## Distortion

Distortion is a preamp device that overdrives your guitar signal prior to it reaching the amp. Settings can be set anywhere from a mild "crunch" to a fully-saturated heavy metal tone. Most distortion pedals include level, tone, and gain settings.

### "Crunch" Rhythm

Settings
Level:    Set at 3 o'clock position
Tone:     Off
Gain:     Set between 8 and 9 o'clock position

### Lead Solo

Settings
Level:    Set between 1 and 2 o'clock position
Tone:     Set at 9 o'clock position
Gain:     Set at 5 o'clock position

## Compressor

Compressors add sustain to a clean signal and typically remain ON. Most compression pedals include level, tone, attack, and sustain settings.

### Country Guitar "Clean"

Settings
Level:     Set at 11 o'clock position
Tone:      Set between 9 – 10 o'clock position
Attack:    Set between 9 – 10 o'clock position
Sustain:   Set at 2 o'clock position

## Signal Chain

When linking pedals between your guitar and amp, their order is extremely important. The following chart depicts a typical layout.

Guitar ----- Compressor ----- Distortion ----- Volume Pedal ----- Delay ----- Amp

While I have found that the above recommended settings and signal chain work well for me, this was arrived at only through many years of playing and experimentation. Remember, no guitar, amp, or effect is a substitute for what's in your hands and heart.

# Appendix A
## Essentials

### Basic Theory

In music, pitches are identified by the first seven letters of the alphabet: A–B–C–D–E–F–G. This is known as the musical alphabet, and within it are two types of consecutive intervals. An *interval* is the distance between two notes. Consecutive intervals are those that proceed to the next letter in the musical alphabet: A to B, B to C, C to D, and so on. This stepwise movement is called *diatonic*, and is the basis for all scales. The further you progress through the musical alphabet, the higher the pitch, until the octave is reached. The octave is the eighth tone above the note started on, and shares the same letter name with that note. Let's examine the two different intervals in our diatonic scale. The diagram shows a combination of whole steps (W) and half steps (H).

On the fretboard these intervals are defined as follows:

Whole Step (W): A two-fret distance in either direction on the same string.

Half Step (H): A one-fret distance in either direction on the same string.

### The Fretboard

Using the open strings as a starting point, we can plot the musical alphabet on the fretboard.

Notice the tones at the twelfth fret have the same letter names as the open strings. At this point all notes on the fretboard repeat an octave higher.

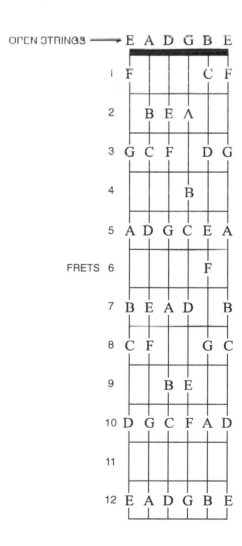

# The Chromatic Scale

Arranging the musical alphabet on the fretboard gives us a good overview of the guitar neck, but it is not complete: we need to name the notes on every fret. By inserting notes between every whole step, we generate a twelve-note scale comprised entirely of half steps. Because we're limited to only seven letters when identifying pitches, we must apply accidentals. An *accidental* is the term for a sharp (♯) or flat (♭).

  The sharp (♯) raises the pitch of a note by a half step (one fret).

  The flat (♭) lowers the pitch of a note by a half step (one fret).

Using accidentals, we can generate a scale made up entirely of half steps. This is called the chromatic scale.

A  A♯  B  C  C♯  D  D♯  E  F  F♯  G  G♯
   or        or     or        or     or
   B♭        D♭     E♭        G♭     A♭

Notice that every sharp (♯) has a flat (♭) equivalent and vice versa. When one pitch shares two names, these names are called *enharmonic*. For example, the enharmonic equivalent of B♭ is A♯, the enharmonic equivalent of D♯ is E♭, and so forth. Here is the completed fretboard diagram, now showing the names of notes on every fret.

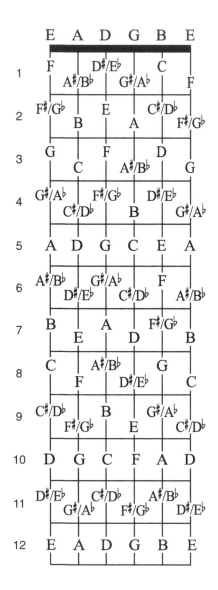

72

# Tuning

The longer you play and progress as a musician the better your ear will become at hearing when something is in tune or out of tune. This is called *relative pitch* and involves distinguishing whether one tone is higher or lower (sharp or flat) in relation to another. Always bring the note up to pitch from below. This means the string should start out slightly flat (or looser), and tightened into pitch with the tuning key. Avoid tuning down to pitch as this can cause string slippage. Tuning requires patience and silence. If you're in a hurry or distracted by other noise, you won't be able to hear whether a note is sharp or flat.

There are several different methods of tuning. The first step is to have a good reference pitch. This is typically an E or A tone and can come from several different sources. If you have a piano or keyboard, match your open sixth string (low E) to the E two octaves below middle C. Tuning forks usually produce an A note from which you can match the open fifth string (A). This is called **A440** and, although two octaves higher, is easy to match to the open A string. Many electronic metronomes are capable of producing A440. You can also get a reference pitch from songs in the key of E or A major. This is particularly helpful when playing with recordings. If you tune the open A string first, the next step is to tune the low E. This is accomplished by comparing the open fifth string A with the A on the fifth fret of the sixth string. They should sound identical.

Once your low E string is in tune we can use the following method to tune the remaining strings.

## Tuning Method

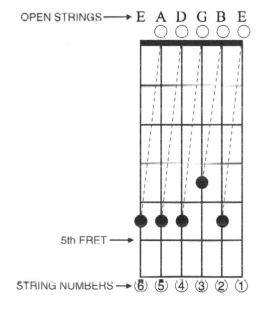

Play the note A on the fifth fret, sixth string. Tune the open fifth string, A, to match this note.

Play the note D on the fifth fret, fifth string. Match this with the open fourth string, D.

Play the note G on the fifth fret, fourth string. Match this with the open third string, G.

Play the note B on the fourth fret, third string. Match this with the open second string, B.

Play the note E on the fifth fret, second string. Match this with the open first string, E.

## Electronic Tuners

Electronic tuners are small meters that read the pitch of an open string. The pitch is then displayed on a screen as flat, sharp, or in tune. Although they can eliminate much of the guesswork, there is no substitute for being able to tune by ear!

# Chord and Scale Diagrams

Scale and chord fingerings are illustrated with grid diagrams, explained below.

## Chord Diagrams

Vertical lines represent strings, and horizontal lines represent frets. The lowest or thickest string (low E) is on the left side, while the highest or thinnest string (high E) is on the right side. Left-hand fingerings are shown as black dots, and the corresponding finger numbers are placed beside them. The root of a chord or scale may be circled. Barres are represented with a curved line, and strings that are not played are shown with an X. With chord diagrams, all fingers are placed down at the same time.

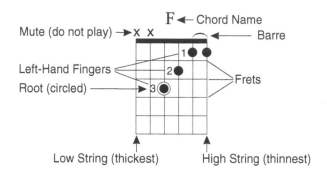

## Scale Diagrams

Scale diagrams are identical to chord diagrams except there are multiple notes per string. When playing through a scale diagram, start with the lowest note on the lowest string. Play all notes shown before repeating the process on the next string. The fret is indicated to the right of the diagram for higher positions. With scale diagrams, all tones are shown but the fingers are placed down sequentially (one at a time). Here is a two-octave C major scale in seventh position.

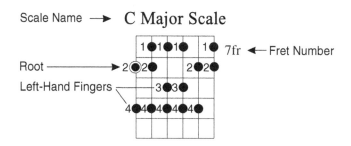

# The Staff

Music is written by placing notes on a *staff*. The musical staff consists of five lines and four spaces. Each line and space represents a letter from the musical alphabet. The higher a note is placed, the higher the pitch. The lower a note is placed, the lower the pitch. The *clef* appears at the beginning of every staff and indicates where the musical alphabet is assigned. Guitar music is written in treble (G) clef. The loop encircles the second line of the staff, designating this as G. From this, we can determine the note names on the remaining lines and spaces.

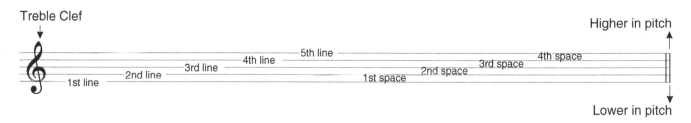

Notes can be written above and below the staff using *ledger lines*.

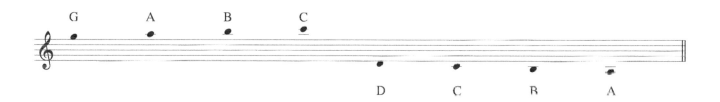

The following shows the location of notes from the open sixth string, E, to the E on the twelfth fret of the first string.

Think of the staff as a "pitch staircase," in which the lines and spaces are steps that continuously ascend or descend through the musical alphabet.

# Rhythm and Counting

The staff is divided into *measures*. Measures are defined as equal groupings of time. Each is separated by a vertical line called a *bar line*. To track progress through the measure, we use beats or counts. It is most common to have four beats per measure. These counts are evenly spaced throughout, and the rate at which the beats are counted is called the *tempo*.

## Note Values

While the location of a note on the staff tells you its pitch, the duration (or value) is indicated by its shape. Below are five note values with the counting for each shown below the measure. Notice that each successive note value is half the length of the previous one.

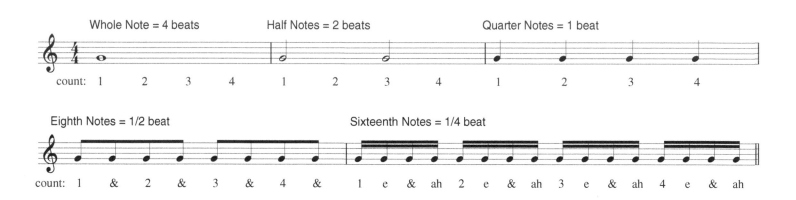

## Time Signature

The time signature appears after the clef at the beginning of a piece of music. The top number indicates the number of beats per measure, while the bottom number indicates which type of note (half, quarter, or eighth) receives one count.

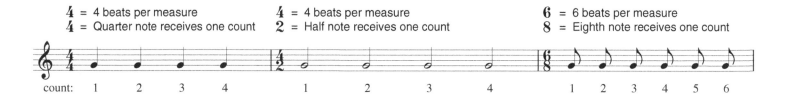

76

# Tablature

Tablature is another system that graphically represents the fretboard. Together with standard notation (staff), tab accurately translates pitch, rhythm, fingering, and location.

## Reading Tablature

- Lines represent strings (low E on bottom, high E on top).
- Numbers represent frets.
- Zero indicates an open string.
- Numbers written separately are played individually as notes.
- Numbers aligned vertically are played together as chords.

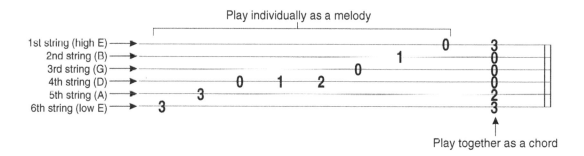

Pitch and rhythm are indicated on the staff above the tablature. Fingerings for both hands and picking direction are also shown. Left-hand fingering is written below the tablature. Right-hand fingering and pick direction are written above the tablature. If chords are present, their symbols are written above the staff.

# Chord Theory and Roman Numerals

Chords are built upon each tone in a seven-note diatonic scale. Roman numerals identify and chart these chords throughout various keys (scales). Below is a C major scale shown with the chords it contains. To represent the location and quality of the chord built upon it, each note or degree is given a roman numeral. In any major scale I, IV, and V are always *major*, ii, iii, and vi are always *minor*, and vii° is of a separate quality called *diminished*. Major chords are identified with upper case (I, IV, and V), and minor and diminished chords use lower case (ii, iii, vi, and vii°). The combination of these chords and notes is called the "key of C major." There are twelve major keys—one for each note in the chromatic scale.

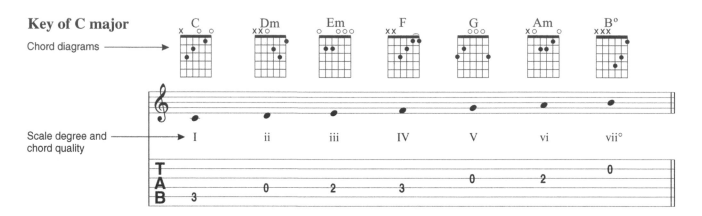

Below are two more harmonized major scales. Note how the same chord types are generated by the new key signatures.

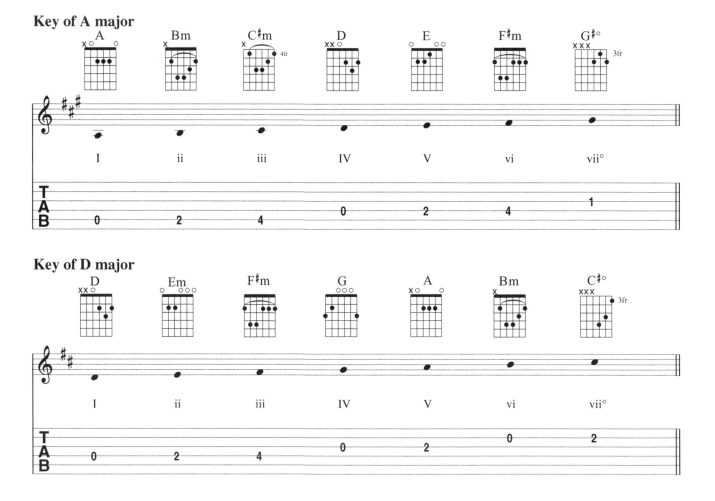

Because chord qualities remain the same in every major key, chord progressions are commonly written using only roman numerals. In this way, a progression can be moved (transposed) from one major key to another. Study how the chords from each key are plugged into the progression.

| Common chord progression (4 measures): | I | vi | IV | V |
|---|---|---|---|---|

| Resulting chords | Key of C major: | C | Am | F | G |
|---|---|---|---|---|---|
| | Key of A major: | A | F♯m | D | E |
| | Key of D major: | D | Bm | G | A |

## Chord Spelling

Major chords are built by taking the root, 3rd, and 5th tones of the major scale. Minor chords are built by taking the root, flatted 3rd, and 5th tones of the major scale. Dominant seventh chords are built by taking the root, 3rd, 5th, and flatted 7th tones of the major scale. In each case, use the major scale whose root matches that of the chord. Here is an example of each formula using C as the root.

| Chord Formulas | C Major Scale |
|---|---|
| Major (1–3–5)<br>Minor (1–♭3–5)<br>Dominant 7th (1–3–5–♭7) | C  D  E  F  G  A  B  C<br>1  2  3  4  5  6  7  8 – Scale Degrees |
| **Resulting Chord (using C as root):** | **Chord Symbol** |
| C major (C–E–G)<br>C minor (C–E♭–G)<br>C seventh (C–E–G–B♭) | C<br>Cm<br>C7 |

# Appendix B
## Essential Listening

I have divided the following recordings into three categories: modern country, classic country, and bluegrass. While this is in no way a comprehensive list, it does reflect those recordings that I consider vital to the development of a player.

## Modern Country

### Albert Lee

Albert Lee & Hogan's Heroes *In Full Flight! (Live at Montreux)* Round Tower Music (RTMCD60)
> Recorded live at the Montreux Jazz Fest; selection highlights include "Country Boy" and "Sweet Little Lisa."

*Speechless* MCA Master Series (MCA5693)
> One of Albert's earlier studio recordings; check out "Bullish Boogie" and the Duane Eddy cover, "Cannonball."

*Gagged But Not Bound* MCA Master Series (MCAC-42063)
> Check out "Fun Ranch Boogie" and "Tiger Rag."

Emmylou Harris *Luxury Liner* Warner Brothers (BSK 3115)
> An absolute classic. The title track is Albert at his finest.

### Ray Flacke

*Untitled Island* Pharaoh Records (Telebender) (B0001N7R1G)
> Hard to find, but full of gems.

Ricky Skaggs *Highways and Heartaches* DCC (B00004R95X)
> Highlights include "Highway 40 Blues" and "Heartbroke."

### Danny Gatton

*The Humbler* NRG Records (#6842)
> Full frontal assault with rockabilly singer Robert Gordon. Check out Danny's solo on "Loverboy."

*Hod Rod Guitar - The Danny Gatton Anthology* Rhino Records (#75691)
> Collection of Gatton's finest works.

*Relentless* with Joey DeFrancesco (Hammond B-3) Big Mo Records (#2023)
> One of my favorite guitar albums. The title says it all.

### Brent Mason

*Hot Wired* Polygram Records (#534782)
> Red hot chickin' pickin' mixed with Carltonesque jazz compositions.

Alan Jackson *A Lot About Livin' (And a Little 'Bout Love)* Arista (#18711)
> The album that put Brent Mason on the map. Hits include "Chattahoochee" and "Mercury Blues."

Mark O'Connor *The New Nashville Cats* Warner Brothers (#26509)
> Another personal favorite. Brent lets loose on "Pick It Apart."

### Reggie Young

*Among Friends* Hush Entertainment (#6617)
> Reggie at his soulful best.

Various Artists *Rhythm Country and Blues* MCA Nashville (#10965)
> Reggie backs a collection of contemporary artists covering R&B classics.

### Pete Anderson

Dwight Yoakam *Hillbilly Deluxe* Warner Brothers (#25567)
> "Tele Twang" at its best. Check out "Little Sister" and "Please, Please Baby."

Dwight Yoakam *Guitars, Cadillacs, Etc., Etc.* Warner Brothers (#25372)

Dig the cool pedal steel licks on Pete's second solo in "Guitars, Cadillacs."

Dwight Yoakam *Dwight Live* Warner Brothers (#45907)

"Bakersfield"-influenced country at its finest. Pete is a master of blending blues and country guitar styles.

## Johnny Hiland

*Johnny Hiland* Favored Nations (B0002JUX6U)

This debut release shows Johnny's fast, articulate, and melodic style in all its glory. Hiland is a true phenomenon and one of my favorite guitarists.

The Don Kelly Band *Everybody's Talking*

Although only available at Robert's Western World in Nashville, where The Don Kelly Band is the house band, this CD is definitely worth tracking down. Highlights include "Truck Driving Man" and "Orange Blossom Special."

## Redd Volkaert

*No Stranger to a Tele* Hightone (B00005A09U)

Although best known as Merle Haggard's guitarist, both of these solo releases pack plenty of punch. Redd is an amazing player, definitely check him out!

*Telewacker* HMG Records (#3002)

## Jimmy Olander

Diamond Rio *Diamond Rio* Arista (#8673)

Jimmy uses both a G and B string bender which make for some real "ear-opening" bends! Check out the instrumental "Poultry Promenade."

## The Hellecasters

*Return of the Hellecasters* Pharaoh (#7001)

John Jorgenson, Jerry Donahue, and Will Ray make up this Telecaster "Trio of Doom." Tele abuse abounds on several originals and covers including "Highlander Boogie" and "Orange Blossom Special."

## Scotty Anderson

*Triple Stop* J-Curve Records (B00005A0LT)

Scotty's unique style blends double and triple stops together with "slippery" chromatic jazz lines. Brilliant playing that will leave you shaking your head in disbelief!

## Jerry Donahue

*Telecasting Recast* Pharaoh (#7004)

Former Richard Thompson sideman and member of The Hellecasters, Jerry throws down some serious chops on this recording! Check out his beautiful ballad "King Arthur's Dream" and the Jerry Reed classic "The Claw."

## Various Artists

*Nashville Guitars* Lightyear (B00004WF31)

This showcase of Nashville's hottest guitar players includes instrumentals from Jimmy Olander, Kelly Black, Tom Hemby, Mark Casstevens, Reggie Young, Dug Grieves, Ray Flacke, Boomer Castleman, Kerry Marx, Johnny Hiland, and Louie Shelton.

# Classic Country

## Jimmy Bryant

*Stratosphere Boogie: The Flaming Guitars of Speedy West and Jimmy Bryant* Razor & Tie (#82067)

Mind-boggling, fast single-note runs. Played super clean and ultra hip!!!

## Roy Nichols

Merle Haggard *Okie from Muskogee* (Live) Capitol (B00005QD81)

This recording from the late sixties captures Roy's great tone and feel. Listen to his solo in "Workin' Man Blues."

## Don Rich

Don Rich & the Buckaroos *Country Pickin': The Don Rich Anthology* Sundazed Music (B0000560ES)

Together with Buck Owens, Don Rich pioneered the "Bakersfield Sound." This collection features many of his finest performances.

Buck Owens *The Very Best of Buck Owens, Vol. 1* Rhino Records (#71816)

A more traditional setting for Don and the Buckaroos.

### Jerry Reed

*The Essential Jerry Reed* RCA (#66592)

Jerry is a complete original. His fingerstyle technique involves tricky independent bass lines and contrary motion. Many players, including myself, are mystified by his unique approach.

### Clarence White

The Byrds *Live at the Filmore West February 1969* Sony (B00004OCE7)

Clarence was co-inventor of the B-Bender. His playing in these country/rock formats was way ahead of its time.

Nashville West *Nashville West* (Live) Hollywood Records (#167000)

### James Burton

*The Guitar Sounds of James Burton* Universal International (B000024R2T)

James has played with everyone from Elvis to Emmylou Harris. This recording features some outstanding playing from an often overlooked innovator of early rock and country guitar.

# Bluegrass

### Doc Watson

*Foundation: Doc Watson Guitar Instrumental Collecton* Sugarhill (B00004U1G6)

Authentic instrumental bluegrass played by one of the best.

Flatt & Scruggs with Doc Watson *Strictly Instrumental* County Records (#117)

Doc joined by two bluegrass originators for a great set of instrumentals.

### Tony Rice

*Manzanita* Rounder (#610092)

My favorite bluegrass guitar recording, Tony Rice is an exceptional arranger and guitarist. Check out the title track (composed by Tony).

*58957: Bluegrass Guitar Collection* Rounder (B0000E3330)

A great collection that showcases Tony's phenomenal chops and sense of melody.

# Guitar Notation Legend

Guitar Music can be notated three different ways: on a *musical staff*, in *tablature*, and in *rhythm slashes*.

**RHYTHM SLASHES** are written above the staff. Strum chords in the rhythm indicated. Use the chord diagrams found at the top of the first page of the transcription for the appropriate chord voicings. Round noteheads indicate single notes.

**THE MUSICAL STAFF** shows pitches and rhythms and is divided by bar lines into measures. Pitches are named after the first seven letters of the alphabet.

**TABLATURE** graphically represents the guitar fingerboard. Each horizontal line represents a a string, and each number represents a fret.

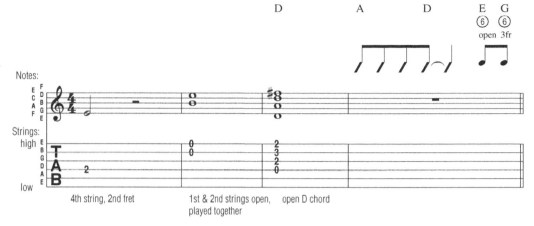

4th string, 2nd fret    1st & 2nd strings open, played together    open D chord

# Definitions for Special Guitar Notation

**HALF-STEP BEND:** Strike the note and bend up 1/2 step.

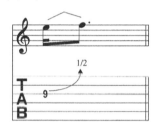

**WHOLE-STEP BEND:** Strike the note and bend up one step.

**GRACE NOTE BEND:** Strike the note and immediately bend up as indicated.

**SLIGHT (MICROTONE) BEND:** Strike the note and bend up 1/4 step.

**BEND AND RELEASE:** Strike the note and bend up as indicated, then release back to the original note. Only the first note is struck.

**PRE-BEND:** Bend the note as indicated, then strike it.

**PRE-BEND AND RELEASE:** Bend the note as indicated. Strike it and release the bend back to the original note.

**UNISON BEND:** Strike the two notes simultaneously and bend the lower note up to the pitch of the higher.

**VIBRATO:** The string is vibrated by rapidly bending and releasing the note with the fretting hand.

**WIDE VIBRATO:** The pitch is varied to a greater degree by vibrating with the fretting hand.

**HAMMER-ON:** Strike the first (lower) note with one finger, then sound the higher note (on the same string) with another finger by fretting it without picking.

**PULL-OFF:** Place both fingers on the notes to be sounded. Strike the first note and without picking, pull the finger off to sound the second (lower) note.

**LEGATO SLIDE:** Strike the first note and then slide the same fret-hand finger up or down to the second note. The second note is not struck.

**SHIFT SLIDE:** Same as legato slide, except the second note is struck.

**TRILL:** Very rapidly alternate between the notes indicated by continuously hammering on and pulling off.

**TAPPING:** Hammer ("tap") the fret indicated with the pick-hand index or middle finger and pull off to the note fretted by the fret hand.

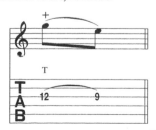

83

**NATURAL HARMONIC:** Strike the note while the fret-hand lightly touches the string directly over the fret indicated.

**PINCH HARMONIC:** The note is fretted normally and a harmonic is produced by adding the edge of the thumb or the tip of the index finger of the pick hand to the normal pick attack.

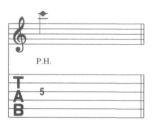

**HARP HARMONIC:** The note is fretted normally and a harmonic is produced by gently resting the pick hand's index finger directly above the indicated fret (in parentheses) while the pick hand's thumb or pick assists by plucking the appropriate string.

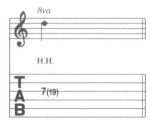

**PICK SCRAPE:** The edge of the pick is rubbed down (or up) the string, producing a scratchy sound.

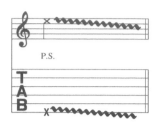

**MUFFLED STRINGS:** A percussive sound is produced by laying the fret hand across the string(s) without depressing, and striking them with the pick hand.

**PALM MUTING:** The note is partially muted by the pick hand lightly touching the string(s) just before the bridge.

**RAKE:** Drag the pick across the strings indicated with a single motion.

**TREMOLO PICKING:** The note is picked as rapidly and continuously as possible.

**ARPEGGIATE:** Play the notes of the chord indicated by quickly rolling them from bottom to top.

**VIBRATO BAR DIVE AND RETURN:** The pitch of the note or chord is dropped a specified number of steps (in rhythm) then returned to the original pitch.

**VIBRATO BAR SCOOP:** Depress the bar just before striking the note, then quickly release the bar.

**VIBRATO BAR DIP:** Strike the note and then immediately drop a specified number of steps, then release back to the original pitch.

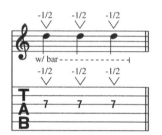

# Additional Musical Definitions

| | | |
|---|---|---|
| > (accent) | • Accentuate note (play it louder) | |
| ∧ (accent) | • Accentuate note with great intensity | |
| • (staccato) | • Play the note short | |
| ⊓ | • Downstroke | |
| ∨ | • Upstroke | |

**Rhy. Fig.** • Label used to recall a recurring accompaniment pattern (usually chordal).

**Riff** • Label used to recall composed, melodic lines (usually single notes) which recur.

**Fill** • Label used to identify a brief melodic figure which is to be inserted into the arrangement.

**Rhy. Fill** • A chordal version of a Fill.

**tacet** • Instrument is silent (drops out).

**D.S. al Coda** • Go back to the sign ( 𝄋 ), then play until the measure marked "*To Coda*," then skip to the section labelled "**Coda**."

**D.C. al Fine** • Go back to the beginning of the song and play until the measure marked "*Fine*" (end).

 • Repeat measures between signs.

 • When a repeated section has different endings, play the first ending only the first time and the second ending only the second time.

**NOTE:** Tablature numbers in parentheses mean:
1. The note is being sustained over a system (note in standard notation is tied), or
2. The note is sustained, but a new articulation (such as a hammer-on, pull-off, slide or vibrato begins), or
3. The note is a barely audible "ghost" note (note in standard notation is also in parentheses).

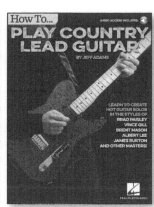
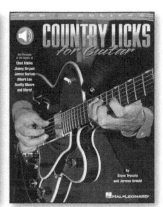

# Guitar Instruction
# Country Style!
## from Hal Leonard

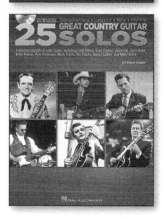

### CHICKEN PICKIN' • by Eric Halbig

This book provides a "bird's-eye-view" of the techniques and licks common to playing hot, country lead guitar! Covers over 100 hot country guitar licks: open-string licks, double-stop licks, scales, string bending, repetitive sequences, and chromatic licks. The online audio includes 99 demonstration tracks with each lick performed at two tempos.

00695599 Book/Online Audio.................................................$17.99

### DANIEL DONATO – THE NEW MASTER OF THE TELECASTER

PATHWAYS TO DYNAMIC SOLOS

This exclusive instructional book and DVD set includes guitar lessons taught by young Nashville phenom Daniel Donato. The "New Master of the Telecaster" shows you his unique "pathways" concept, opening your mind and fingers to uninhibited fretboard freedom, increased music theory comprehension, and more dynamic solos! The DVD features Daniel Donato himself providing full-band performances and a full hour of guitar lessons. The book includes guitar tab for all the DVD lessons and performances. Topics covered include: using chromatic notes • application of bends • double stops • analyzing different styles • and more. DVD running time: 1 hr., 4 min.

00121923 Book/DVD Pack .........................................................$19.99

### FRETBOARD ROADMAPS – COUNTRY GUITAR

The Essential Patterns That All the Pros Know and Use • by Fred Sokolow

This book/CD pack will teach you how to play lead and rhythm in the country style anywhere on the fretboard in any key. You'll play basic country progressions, boogie licks, steel licks, and other melodies and licks. You'll also learn a variety of lead guitar styles using moveable scale patterns, sliding scale patterns, chord-based licks, double-note licks, and more. The book features easy-to-follow diagrams and instructions for beginning, intermediate, and advanced players.

00695353 Book/CD Pack.............................................................$15.99

### HOW TO PLAY COUNTRY LEAD GUITAR

by Jeff Adams

Here is a comprehensive stylistic breakdown of country guitar techniques from the past 50 years. Drawing inspiration from the timelessly innovative licks of Merle Travis, Chet Atkins, Albert Lee, Vince Gill, Brent Mason and Brad Paisley, the near 90 musical examples within these pages will hone your left and right hands with technical string-bending and rolling licks while sharpening your knowledge of the thought process behind creating your own licks, and why and when to play them.

00131103 Book/Online Audio.....................................................$19.99

### COUNTRY LICKS FOR GUITAR

by Steve Trovato and Jerome Arnold

This unique package examines the lead guitar licks of the masters of country guitar, such as Chet Atkins, Jimmy Bryant, James Burton, Albert Lee, Scotty Moore, and many others! The online audio includes demonstrations of each lick at normal and slow speeds. The instruction covers single-string licks, pedal-steel licks, open-string licks, chord licks, rockabilly licks, funky country licks, tips on fingerings, phrasing, technique, and application.

00695577 Book/Online Audo.............................$17.99

### COUNTRY SOLOS FOR GUITAR

by Steve Trovato

This unique book/audio pack lets guitarists examine the solo styles of axe masters such as Chet Atkins, James Burton, Ray Flacke, Albert Lee, Scotty Moore, Roy Nichols, Jerry Reed and others. It covers techniques including hot banjo rolls, funky double stops, pedal-steel licks, open-string licks and more, in standard notation and tab with phrase-by-phrase performance notes. The online audio includes full demonstrations and rhythm-only tracks.

00695448 Book/Online Audio............................$17.99

### RED-HOT COUNTRY GUITAR

by Michael Hawley

The complete guide to playing lead guitar in the styles of Pete Anderson, Danny Gatton, Albert Lee, Brent Mason, and more. Includes loads of red-hot licks, techniques, solos, theory and more.

00695831 Book/Online Audio..................................................................$17.99

### 25 GREAT COUNTRY GUITAR SOLOS

by Dave Rubin

Provides solo transcriptions in notes & tab, lessons on how to play them, guitarist bios, equipment notes, photos, history, and much more. The CD contains full-band demos of every solo in the book. Songs include: Country Boy • Foggy Mountain Special • Folsom Prison Blues • Hellecaster Theme • Hello Mary Lou • I've Got a Tiger by the Tail • The Only Daddy That Will Walk the Line • Please, Please Baby • Sugarfoot Rag • and more.

00699926 Book/CD Pack...............................................................................$19.99

## HAL•LEONARD®

**www.halleonard.com**
Prices, contents, and availability subject to change without notice.

0619
183

Signature Licks book/audio packs provide a step-by-step breakdown of "right from the record" riffs, licks, and solos so you can jam along with your favorite bands. They contain performance notes and an overview of each artist's or group's style, with note-for-note transcriptions in notes and tab. The online audio tracks feature full-band demos at both normal and slow speeds.

**AC/DC**
14041352.................................. $22.99

**AEROSMITH 1973-1979**
00695106.................................. $22.95

**AEROSMITH 1979-1998**
00695219.................................. $22.95

**DUANE ALLMAN**
00696042.................................. $22.99

**BEST OF CHET ATKINS**
00695752.................................. $24.99

**AVENGED SEVENFOLD**
00696473.................................. $22.99

**THE BEATLES**
00298845.................................. $24.99

**BEST OF THE BEATLES FOR ACOUSTIC GUITAR**
00695453.................................. $22.99

**THE BEATLES HITS**
00695049.................................. $24.95

**JEFF BECK**
00696427.................................. $22.99

**BEST OF GEORGE BENSON**
00695418.................................. $22.99

**BEST OF BLACK SABBATH**
00695249.................................. $22.95

**BLUES BREAKERS WITH JOHN MAYALL & ERIC CLAPTON**
00696374.................................. $24.99

**BON JOVI**
00696380.................................. $22.99

**ROY BUCHANAN**
00696654.................................. $22.99

**KENNY BURRELL**
00695830.................................. $24.99

**BEST OF CHARLIE CHRISTIAN**
00695584.................................. $24.99

**BEST OF ERIC CLAPTON**
00695038.................................. $24.99

**ERIC CLAPTON – FROM THE ALBUM UNPLUGGED**
00695250.................................. $24.99

**BEST OF CREAM**
00695251.................................. $22.95

**CREEDANCE CLEARWATER REVIVAL**
00695924.................................. $24.99

**THE DOORS**
00695373.................................. $22.95

**DEEP PURPLE – GREATEST HITS**
00695625.................................. $22.99

**DREAM THEATER**
00111943.................................. $24.99

**TOMMY EMMANUEL**
00696409.................................. $22.99

**ESSENTIAL JAZZ GUITAR**
00695875.................................. $19.99

**FAMOUS ROCK GUITAR SOLOS**
00695590.................................. $19.95

**FLEETWOOD MAC**
00696416.................................. $22.99

**BEST OF FOO FIGHTERS**
00695481.................................. $24.95

**ROBBEN FORD**
00695903.................................. $22.95

**BEST OF GRANT GREEN**
00695747.................................. $22.99

**PETER GREEN**
00145386.................................. $22.99

**BEST OF GUNS N' ROSES**
00695183.................................. $24.99

**THE BEST OF BUDDY GUY**
00695186.................................. $22.99

**JIM HALL**
00695848.................................. $29.99

**JIMI HENDRIX**
00696560.................................. $24.99

**JIMI HENDRIX – VOLUME 2**
00695835.................................. $24.99

**JOHN LEE HOOKER**
00695894.................................. $22.99

**BEST OF JAZZ GUITAR**
00695586.................................. $29.99

**ERIC JOHNSON**
00699317.................................. $24.99

**ROBERT JOHNSON**
00695264.................................. $24.99

**BARNEY KESSEL**
00696009.................................. $24.99

**THE ESSENTIAL ALBERT KING**
00695713.................................. $24.99

**B.B. KING – BLUES LEGEND**
00696039.................................. $22.99

**B.B. KING – THE DEFINITIVE COLLECTION**
00695635.................................. $22.99

**MARK KNOPFLER**
00695178.................................. $24.99

**LYNYRD SKYNYRD**
00695872.................................. $24.99

**THE BEST OF YNGWIE MALMSTEEN**
00695669.................................. $24.99

**BEST OF PAT MARTINO**
00695632.................................. $24.99

**MEGADETH**
00696421.................................. $22.99

**WES MONTGOMERY**
00695387.................................. $24.99

**BEST OF NIRVANA**
00695483.................................. $24.95

**VERY BEST OF OZZY OSBOURNE**
00695431.................................. $22.99

**BRAD PAISLEY**
00696379.................................. $22.99

**BEST OF JOE PASS**
00695730.................................. $22.99

**TOM PETTY**
00696021.................................. $22.99

**PINK FLOYD**
00103659.................................. $24.99

**THE GUITAR OF ELVIS**
00174800.................................. $22.99

**BEST OF QUEEN**
00695097.................................. $24.99

**RADIOHEAD**
00109304.................................. $24.99

**BEST OF RAGE AGAINST THE MACHINE**
00695480.................................. $24.95

**RED HOT CHILI PEPPERS**
00695173.................................. $22.95

**RED HOT CHILI PEPPERS – GREATEST HITS**
00695828.................................. $24.99

**JERRY REED**
00118236.................................. $22.99

**BEST OF DJANGO REINHARDT**
00695660.................................. $24.99

**BEST OF ROCK 'N' ROLL GUITAR**
00695559.................................. $22.99

**BEST OF ROCKABILLY GUITAR**
00695785.................................. $19.99

**BEST OF CARLOS SANTANA**
00174664.................................. $22.99

**BEST OF JOE SATRIANI**
00695216.................................. $22.95

**SLASH**
00696576.................................. $22.99

**SLAYER**
00121281.................................. $22.99

**THE BEST OF SOUL GUITAR**
00695703.................................. $19.95

**BEST OF SOUTHERN ROCK**
00695560.................................. $19.95

**STEELY DAN**
00696015.................................. $22.99

**MIKE STERN**
00695800.................................. $24.99

**BEST OF SURF GUITAR**
00695822.................................. $19.95

**STEVE VAI**
00673247.................................. $24.99

**STEVE VAI – ALIEN LOVE SECRETS: THE NAKED VAMPS**
00695223.................................. $22.95

**STEVE VAI – FIRE GARDEN: THE NAKED VAMPS**
00695166.................................. $22.95

**STEVE VAI – THE ULTRA ZONE: NAKED VAMPS**
00695684.................................. $22.95

**VAN HALEN**
00110227.................................. $24.99

**STEVIE RAY VAUGHAN – 2ND ED.**
00699316.................................. $24.95

**THE GUITAR STYLE OF STEVIE RAY VAUGHAN**
00695155.................................. $24.95

**BEST OF THE VENTURES**
00695772.................................. $19.95

**THE WHO – 2ND ED.**
00695561.................................. $22.99

**JOHNNY WINTER**
00695951.................................. $24.99

**YES**
00113120.................................. $22.99

**NEIL YOUNG – GREATEST HITS**
00695988.................................. $22.99

**BEST OF ZZ TOP**
00695738.................................. $24.99

HAL•LEONARD®

www.halleonard.com

**COMPLETE DESCRIPTIONS AND SONGLISTS ONLINE!**
Prices, contents and availability subject to change without notice.

0720
305

# RECORDED VERSIONS®

## The Best Note-For-Note Transcriptions Available

**AUTHENTIC TRANSCRIPTIONS WITH NOTES AND TABLATURE**

| | | |
|---|---|---|
| 00690603 | Aerosmith – O Yeah! Ultimate Hits | $27.99 |
| 00690178 | Alice in Chains – Acoustic | $19.99 |
| 00694865 | Alice in Chains – Dirt | $19.99 |
| 00694925 | Alice in Chains – Jar of Flies/Sap | $19.99 |
| 00691091 | Alice Cooper – Best of | $24.99 |
| 00690958 | Duane Allman – Guitar Anthology | $29.99 |
| 00694932 | Allman Brothers Band – Volume 1 | $27.99 |
| 00694933 | Allman Brothers Band – Volume 2 | $24.99 |
| 00694934 | Allman Brothers Band – Volume 3 | $24.99 |
| 00690945 | Alter Bridge – Blackbird | $24.99 |
| 00123558 | Arctic Monkeys – AM | $24.99 |
| 00214869 | Avenged Sevenfold – Best of 2005-2013 | $24.99 |
| 00690489 | Beatles – 1 | $24.99 |
| 00694929 | Beatles – 1962-1966 | $24.99 |
| 00694930 | Beatles – 1967-1970 | $27.99 |
| 00694880 | Beatles – Abbey Road | $19.99 |
| 00694832 | Beatles – Acoustic Guitar | $24.99 |
| 00690110 | Beatles – White Album (Book 1) | $19.99 |
| 00692385 | Chuck Berry | $22.99 |
| 00147707 | Black Crowes – Best of | $19.99 |
| 00690149 | Black Sabbath | $17.99 |
| 00690901 | Black Sabbath – Best of | $22.99 |
| 00691010 | Black Sabbath – Heaven and Hell | $22.99 |
| 00090140 | Black Sabbath – Master of Reality | $17.99 |
| 00690142 | Black Sabbath – Paranoid | $16.99 |
| 00148544 | Michael Bloomfield – Guitar Anthology | $24.99 |
| 00158600 | Joe Bonamassa – Blues of Desperation | $22.99 |
| 00198117 | Joe Bonamassa – Muddy Wolf at Red Rocks | $24.99 |
| 00283540 | Joe Bonamassa – Redemption | $24.99 |
| 00690913 | Boston | $19.99 |
| 00690491 | David Bowie – Best of | $19.99 |
| 00286503 | Big Bill Broonzy – Guitar Collection | $19.99 |
| 00690261 | The Carter Family Collection | $19.99 |
| 00691079 | Johnny Cash – Best of | $22.99 |
| 00690936 | Eric Clapton – Complete Clapton | $29.99 |
| 00694869 | Eric Clapton – Unplugged | $24.99 |
| 00124873 | Eric Clapton – Unplugged (Deluxe) | $27.99 |
| 00138731 | Eric Clapton & Friends – The Breeze | $22.99 |
| 00139967 | Coheed & Cambria – In Keeping Secrets of Silent Earth: 3 | $24.99 |
| 00141704 | Jesse Cook – Works, Vol. 1 | $19.99 |
| 00288787 | Creed – Greatest Hits | $22.99 |
| 00690819 | Creedence Clearwater Revival | $24.99 |
| 00690648 | Jim Croce – Very Best of | $19.99 |
| 00690572 | Steve Cropper – Soul Man | $19.99 |
| 00690613 | Crosby, Stills & Nash – Best of | $27.99 |
| 00690784 | Def Leppard – Best of | $22.99 |
| 00695831 | Derek and the Dominos – Layla & Other Assorted Love Songs | $24.99 |
| 00291164 | Dream Theater – Distance Over Time | $24.99 |
| 00278631 | Eagles – Greatest Hits 1971-1975 | $22.99 |
| 00278632 | Eagles – Very Best of | $34.99 |
| 00690515 | Extreme II – Pornograffiti | $24.99 |
| 00150257 | John Fahey – Guitar Anthology | $19.99 |
| 00690664 | Fleetwood Mac – Best of | $24.99 |
| 00691024 | Foo Fighters – Greatest Hits | $22.99 |
| 00120220 | Robben Ford – Guitar Anthology | $29.99 |
| 00295410 | Rory Gallagher – Blues | $24.99 |
| 00139460 | Grateful Dead – Guitar Anthology | $24.99 |

| | | |
|---|---|---|
| 00691190 | Peter Green – Best of | $24.99 |
| 00287517 | Greta Van Fleet – Anthem of the Peaceful Army | $19.99 |
| 00287515 | Greta Van Fleet – From the Fires | $19.99 |
| 00694798 | George Harrison – Anthology | $22.99 |
| 00692930 | Jimi Hendrix – Are You Experienced? | $27.99 |
| 00692931 | Jimi Hendrix – Axis: Bold As Love | $24.99 |
| 00690304 | Jimi Hendrix – Band of Gypsys | $24.99 |
| 00694944 | Jimi Hendrix – Blues | $27.99 |
| 00692932 | Jimi Hendrix – Electric Ladyland | $27.99 |
| 00660029 | Buddy Holly – Best of | $22.99 |
| 00200446 | Iron Maiden – Guitar Tab | $29.99 |
| 00694912 | Eric Johnson – Ah Via Musicom | $24.99 |
| 00690271 | Robert Johnson – Transcriptions | $24.99 |
| 00690427 | Judas Priest – Best of | $24.99 |
| 00130447 | B.B. King – Live at the Regal | $10.00 |
| 00690492 | B.B. King – Anthology | $24.99 |
| 00690134 | Freddie King – Collection | $19.99 |
| 00327968 | Marcus King – El Dorado | $22.99 |
| 00690157 | Kiss – Alive | $19.99 |
| 00690356 | Kiss – Alive II | $22.99 |
| 00291163 | Kiss – Very Best of | $22.99 |
| 00690377 | Kris Kristofferson – Guitar Collection | $19.99 |
| 00690834 | Lamb of God – Ashes of the Wake | $24.99 |
| 00690525 | George Lynch – Best of | $24.99 |
| 00690955 | Lynyrd Skynyrd – All-Time Greatest Hits | $24.99 |
| 00694954 | Lynyrd Skynyrd – New Best of | $24.99 |
| 00690577 | Yngwie Malmsteen – Anthology | $29.99 |
| 00694896 | John Mayall with Eric Clapton – Blues Breakers | $19.99 |
| 00694952 | Megadeth – Countdown to Extinction | $24.99 |
| 00276065 | Megadeth – Greatest Hits: Back to the Start | $24.99 |
| 00694951 | Megadeth – Rust in Peace | $24.99 |
| 00690011 | Megadeth – Youthanasia | $24.99 |
| 00209876 | Metallica – Hardwired to Self-Destruct | $22.99 |
| 00690646 | Pat Metheny – One Quiet Night | $22.99 |
| 00102591 | Wes Montgomery – Guitar Anthology | $24.99 |
| 00691092 | Gary Moore – Best of | $24.99 |
| 00694802 | Gary Moore – Still Got the Blues | $24.99 |
| 00355456 | Alanis Morisette – Jagged Little Pill | $22.99 |
| 00690611 | Nirvana | $22.95 |
| 00694913 | Nirvana – In Utero | $19.99 |
| 00694883 | Nirvana – Nevermind | $19.99 |
| 00690026 | Nirvana – Unplugged in New York | $19.99 |
| 00265439 | Nothing More – Tab Collection | $24.99 |
| 00243349 | Opeth – Best of | $22.99 |
| 00690499 | Tom Petty – Definitive Guitar Collection | $19.99 |
| 00121933 | Pink Floyd – Acoustic Guitar Collection | $24.99 |
| 00690428 | Pink Floyd – Dark Side of the Moon | $19.99 |
| 00244637 | Pink Floyd – Guitar Anthology | $24.99 |
| 00239799 | Pink Floyd – The Wall | $24.99 |
| 00690789 | Poison – Best of | $19.99 |
| 00690625 | Prince – Very Best of | $22.99 |
| 00690003 | Queen – Classic Queen | $24.99 |
| 00694975 | Queen – Greatest Hits | $25.99 |
| 00694910 | Rage Against the Machine | $22.99 |
| 00119834 | Rage Against the Machine – Guitar Anthology | $24.99 |

| | | |
|---|---|---|
| 00690426 | Ratt – Best of | $19.95 |
| 00690055 | Red Hot Chili Peppers – Blood Sugar Sex Magik | $19.99 |
| 00690379 | Red Hot Chili Peppers – Californication | $19.99 |
| 00690673 | Red Hot Chili Peppers – Greatest Hits | $22.99 |
| 00690852 | Red Hot Chili Peppers – Stadium Arcadium | $27.99 |
| 00690511 | Django Reinhardt – Definitive Collection | $22.99 |
| 00690014 | Rolling Stones – Exile on Main Street | $24.99 |
| 00690631 | Rolling Stones – Guitar Anthology | $29.99 |
| 00323854 | Rush – The Spirit of Radio: Greatest Hits, 1974-1987 | $22.99 |
| 00173534 | Santana – Guitar Anthology | $27.99 |
| 00276350 | Joe Satriani – What Happens Next | $24.00 |
| 00690566 | Scorpions – Best of | $24.99 |
| 00690604 | Bob Seger – Guitar Collection | $24.99 |
| 00234543 | Ed Sheeran – Divide* | $19.99 |
| 00691114 | Slash – Guitar Anthology | $29.99 |
| 00690813 | Slayer – Guitar Collection | $19.99 |
| 00690419 | Slipknot | $19.99 |
| 00316982 | Smashing Pumpkins – Greatest Hits | $22.99 |
| 00690912 | Soundgarden – Guitar Anthology | $24.99 |
| 00120004 | Steely Dan – Best of | $24.99 |
| 00120081 | Sublime | $19.99 |
| 00690531 | System of a Down – Toxicity | $19.99 |
| 00694824 | James Taylor – Best of | $19.99 |
| 00694887 | Thin Lizzy – Best of | $19.99 |
| 00253237 | Trivium – Guitar Tab Anthology | $24.99 |
| 00690683 | Robin Trower – Bridge of Sighs | $19.99 |
| 00156024 | Steve Vai – Guitar Anthology | $34.99 |
| 00660137 | Steve Vai – Passion & Warfare | $27.50 |
| 00295076 | Van Halen – 30 Classics | $29.99 |
| 00690024 | Stevie Ray Vaughan – Couldn't Stand the Weather | $19.99 |
| 00660058 | Stevie Ray Vaughan – Lightnin' Blues 1983-1987 | $29.99 |
| 00217455 | Stevie Ray Vaughan – Plays Slow Blues | $19.99 |
| 00694835 | Stevie Ray Vaughan – The Sky Is Crying | $24.99 |
| 00690015 | Stevie Ray Vaughan – Texas Flood | $19.99 |
| 00694789 | Muddy Waters – Deep Blues | $24.99 |
| 00152161 | Doc Watson – Guitar Anthology | $22.99 |
| 00690071 | Weezer (The Blue Album) | $19.99 |
| 00117511 | Whitesnake – Guitar Collection | $22.99 |
| 00122303 | Yes – Guitar Collection | $22.99 |
| 00690443 | Frank Zappa – Hot Rats | $22.99 |
| 00121684 | ZZ Top – Early Classics | $27.99 |
| 00690589 | ZZ Top – Guitar Anthology | $24.99 |

**COMPLETE SERIES LIST ONLINE!**

**HAL•LEONARD®**
www.halleonard.com

Prices and availability subject to change without notice.
*Tab transcriptions only.

This series will help you play your favorite songs quickly and easily. Just follow the tab and listen to the audio to the hear how the guitar should sound, and then play along using the separate backing tracks. Audio files also include software to slow down the tempo without changing pitch. The melody and lyrics are included in the book so that you can sing or simply follow along.

INCLUDES TAB

**Complete song lists available online.**

| | |
|---|---|
| VOL. 1 – ROCK | 00699570 / $16.99 |
| VOL. 2 – ACOUSTIC | 00699569 / $16.99 |
| VOL. 3 – HARD ROCK | 00699573 / $17.99 |
| VOL. 4 – POP/ROCK | 00699571 / $16.99 |
| VOL. 5 – THREE CHORD SONGS | 00300985 / $16.99 |
| VOL. 6 – '90S ROCK | 00298615 / $16.99 |
| VOL. 7 – BLUES | 00699575 / $17.99 |
| VOL. 8 – ROCK | 00699585 / $16.99 |
| VOL. 9 – EASY ACOUSTIC SONGS | 00151708 / $16.99 |
| VOL. 10 – ACOUSTIC | 00699586 / $16.95 |
| VOL. 11 – EARLY ROCK | 00699579 / $15.99 |
| VOL. 12 – ROCK POP | 00291724 / $16.99 |
| VOL. 14 – BLUES ROCK | 00699582 / $16.99 |
| VOL. 15 – R&B | 00699583 / $17.99 |
| VOL. 16 – JAZZ | 00699584 / $15.95 |
| VOL. 17 – COUNTRY | 00699588 / $16.99 |
| VOL. 18 – ACOUSTIC ROCK | 00699577 / $15.95 |
| VOL. 20 – ROCKABILLY | 00699580 / $16.99 |
| VOL. 21 – SANTANA | 00174525 / $17.99 |
| VOL. 22 – CHRISTMAS | 00699600 / $15.99 |
| VOL. 23 – SURF | 00699635 / $16.99 |
| VOL. 24 – ERIC CLAPTON | 00699649 / $17.99 |
| VOL. 25 – THE BEATLES | 00198265 / $17.99 |
| VOL. 26 – ELVIS PRESLEY | 00699643 / $16.99 |
| VOL. 27 – DAVID LEE ROTH | 00699645 / $16.95 |
| VOL. 28 – GREG KOCH | 00699646 / $17.99 |
| VOL. 29 – BOB SEGER | 00699647 / $16.99 |
| VOL. 30 – KISS | 00699644 / $16.99 |
| VOL. 32 – THE OFFSPRING | 00699653 / $14.95 |
| VOL. 33 – ACOUSTIC CLASSICS | 00699656 / $17.99 |
| VOL. 34 – CLASSIC ROCK | 00699658 / $17.99 |
| VOL. 35 – HAIR METAL | 00699660 / $17.99 |
| VOL. 36 – SOUTHERN ROCK | 00699661 / $19.99 |
| VOL. 37 – ACOUSTIC UNPLUGGED | 00699662 / $22.99 |
| VOL. 38 – BLUES | 00699663 / $17.99 |
| VOL. 39 – '80s METAL | 00699664 / $16.99 |
| VOL. 40 – INCUBUS | 00699668 / $17.95 |
| VOL. 41 – ERIC CLAPTON | 00699669 / $17.99 |
| VOL. 42 – COVER BAND HITS | 00211597 / $16.99 |
| VOL. 43 – LYNYRD SKYNYRD | 00699681 / $19.99 |
| VOL. 44 – JAZZ GREATS | 00699689 / $16.99 |
| VOL. 45 – TV THEMES | 00699718 / $14.95 |
| VOL. 46 – MAINSTREAM ROCK | 00699722 / $16.95 |
| VOL. 47 – JIMI HENDRIX SMASH HITS | 00699723 / $19.99 |
| VOL. 48 – AEROSMITH CLASSICS | 00699724 / $17.99 |
| VOL. 49 – STEVIE RAY VAUGHAN | 00699725 / $17.99 |
| VOL. 50 – VAN HALEN: 1978-1984 | 00110269 / $19.99 |
| VOL. 51 – ALTERNATIVE '90s | 00699727 / $14.99 |
| VOL. 52 – FUNK | 00699728 / $15.99 |
| VOL. 53 – DISCO | 00699729 / $14.99 |
| VOL. 54 – HEAVY METAL | 00699730 / $16.99 |
| VOL. 55 – POP METAL | 00699731 / $14.95 |
| VOL. 56 – FOO FIGHTERS | 00699749 / $17.99 |
| VOL. 57 – GUNS 'N' ROSES | 00159922 / $17.99 |
| VOL. 58 – BLINK 182 | 00699772 / $14.95 |
| VOL. 59 – CHET ATKINS | 00702347 / $16.99 |
| VOL. 60 – 3 DOORS DOWN | 00699774 / $14.95 |
| VOL. 62 – CHRISTMAS CAROLS | 00699798 / $12.95 |
| VOL. 63 – CREEDENCE CLEARWATER REVIVAL | 00699802 / $16.99 |
| VOL. 64 – ULTIMATE OZZY OSBOURNE | 00699803 / $17.99 |
| VOL. 66 – THE ROLLING STONES | 00699807 / $17.99 |
| VOL. 67 – BLACK SABBATH | 00699808 / $16.99 |
| VOL. 68 – PINK FLOYD – DARK SIDE OF THE MOON | 00699809 / $16.99 |
| VOL. 71 – CHRISTIAN ROCK | 00699824 / $14.95 |

| | |
|---|---|
| VOL. 72 – ACOUSTIC '90s | 00699827 / $14.95 |
| VOL. 73 – BLUESY ROCK | 00699829 / $16.99 |
| VOL. 74 – SIMPLE STRUMMING SONGS | 00151706 / $19.99 |
| VOL. 75 – TOM PETTY | 00699882 / $17.99 |
| VOL. 76 – COUNTRY HITS | 00699884 / $16.99 |
| VOL. 77 – BLUEGRASS | 00699910 / $15.99 |
| VOL. 78 – NIRVANA | 00700132 / $16.99 |
| VOL. 79 – NEIL YOUNG | 00700133 / $24.99 |
| VOL. 80 – ACOUSTIC ANTHOLOGY | 00700175 / $19.95 |
| VOL. 81 – ROCK ANTHOLOGY | 00700176 / $22.99 |
| VOL. 82 – EASY ROCK SONGS | 00700177 / $17.99 |
| VOL. 84 – STEELY DAN | 00700200 / $19.99 |
| VOL. 85 – THE POLICE | 00700269 / $16.99 |
| VOL. 86 – BOSTON | 00700465 / $16.99 |
| VOL. 87 – ACOUSTIC WOMEN | 00700763 / $14.99 |
| VOL. 88 – GRUNGE | 00700467 / $16.99 |
| VOL. 89 – REGGAE | 00700468 / $15.99 |
| VOL. 90 – CLASSICAL POP | 00700469 / $14.99 |
| VOL. 91 – BLUES INSTRUMENTALS | 00700505 / $17.99 |
| VOL. 92 – EARLY ROCK INSTRUMENTALS | 00700506 / $15.99 |
| VOL. 93 – ROCK INSTRUMENTALS | 00700507 / $16.99 |
| VOL. 94 – SLOW BLUES | 00700508 / $16.99 |
| VOL. 95 – BLUES CLASSICS | 00700509 / $15.99 |
| VOL. 96 – BEST COUNTRY HITS | 00211615 / $16.99 |
| VOL. 97 – CHRISTMAS CLASSICS | 00236542 / $14.99 |
| VOL. 98 – ROCK BAND | 00700704 / $14.95 |
| VOL. 99 – ZZ TOP | 00700762 / $16.99 |
| VOL. 100 – B.B. KING | 00700466 / $16.99 |
| VOL. 101 – SONGS FOR BEGINNERS | 00701917 / $14.99 |
| VOL. 102 – CLASSIC PUNK | 00700769 / $14.99 |
| VOL. 103 – SWITCHFOOT | 00700773 / $16.99 |
| VOL. 104 – DUANE ALLMAN | 00700846 / $17.99 |
| VOL. 105 – LATIN | 00700939 / $16.99 |
| VOL. 106 – WEEZER | 00700958 / $14.99 |
| VOL. 107 – CREAM | 00701069 / $16.99 |
| VOL. 108 – THE WHO | 00701053 / $16.99 |
| VOL. 109 – STEVE MILLER | 00701054 / $19.99 |
| VOL. 110 – SLIDE GUITAR HITS | 00701055 / $16.99 |
| VOL. 111 – JOHN MELLENCAMP | 00701056 / $14.99 |
| VOL. 112 – QUEEN | 00701052 / $16.99 |
| VOL. 113 – JIM CROCE | 00701058 / $17.99 |
| VOL. 114 – BON JOVI | 00701060 / $16.99 |
| VOL. 115 – JOHNNY CASH | 00701070 / $16.99 |
| VOL. 116 – THE VENTURES | 00701124 / $16.99 |
| VOL. 117 – BRAD PAISLEY | 00701224 / $16.99 |
| VOL. 118 – ERIC JOHNSON | 00701353 / $16.99 |
| VOL. 119 – AC/DC CLASSICS | 00701356 / $17.99 |
| VOL. 120 – PROGRESSIVE ROCK | 00701457 / $14.99 |
| VOL. 121 – U2 | 00701508 / $16.99 |
| VOL. 122 – CROSBY, STILLS & NASH | 00701610 / $16.99 |
| VOL. 123 – LENNON & McCARTNEY ACOUSTIC | 00701614 / $16.99 |
| VOL. 124 – SMOOTH JAZZ | 00200664 / $16.99 |
| VOL. 125 – JEFF BECK | 00701687 / $17.99 |
| VOL. 126 – BOB MARLEY | 00701701 / $16.99 |
| VOL. 127 – 1970s ROCK | 00701739 / $16.99 |
| VOL. 128 – 1960s ROCK | 00701740 / $15.99 |
| VOL. 129 – MEGADETH | 00701741 / $17.99 |
| VOL. 130 – IRON MAIDEN | 00701742 / $17.99 |
| VOL. 131 – 1990s ROCK | 00701743 / $14.99 |
| VOL. 132 – COUNTRY ROCK | 00701757 / $15.99 |
| VOL. 133 – TAYLOR SWIFT | 00701894 / $16.99 |
| VOL. 134 – AVENGED SEVENFOLD | 00701906 / $16.99 |
| VOL. 135 – MINOR BLUES | 00151350 / $17.99 |
| VOL. 136 – GUITAR THEMES | 00701922 / $14.99 |
| VOL. 137 – IRISH TUNES | 00701966 / $15.99 |
| VOL. 138 – BLUEGRASS CLASSICS | 00701967 / $17.99 |

| | |
|---|---|
| VOL. 139 – GARY MOORE | 00702370 / $16.99 |
| VOL. 140 – MORE STEVIE RAY VAUGHAN | 00702396 / $17.99 |
| VOL. 141 – ACOUSTIC HITS | 00702401 / $16.99 |
| VOL. 142 – GEORGE HARRISON | 00237697 / $17.99 |
| VOL. 143 – SLASH | 00702425 / $19.99 |
| VOL. 144 – DJANGO REINHARDT | 00702531 / $16.99 |
| VOL. 145 – DEF LEPPARD | 00702532 / $17.99 |
| VOL. 146 – ROBERT JOHNSON | 00702533 / $16.99 |
| VOL. 147 – SIMON & GARFUNKEL | 14041591 / $16.99 |
| VOL. 148 – BOB DYLAN | 14041592 / $16.99 |
| VOL. 149 – AC/DC HITS | 14041593 / $17.99 |
| VOL. 150 – ZAKK WYLDE | 02501717 / $16.99 |
| VOL. 151 – J.S. BACH | 02501730 / $16.99 |
| VOL. 152 – JOE BONAMASSA | 02501751 / $19.99 |
| VOL. 153 – RED HOT CHILI PEPPERS | 00702990 / $19.99 |
| VOL. 154 – GLEE | 00703018 / $16.99 |
| VOL. 155 – ERIC CLAPTON UNPLUGGED | 00703085 / $16.99 |
| VOL. 156 – SLAYER | 00703770 / $19.99 |
| VOL. 157 – FLEETWOOD MAC | 00101382 / $17.99 |
| VOL. 159 – WES MONTGOMERY | 00102593 / $19.99 |
| VOL. 160 – T-BONE WALKER | 00102641 / $17.99 |
| VOL. 161 – THE EAGLES ACOUSTIC | 00102659 / $17.99 |
| VOL. 162 – THE EAGLES HITS | 00102667 / $17.99 |
| VOL. 163 – PANTERA | 00103036 / $17.99 |
| VOL. 164 – VAN HALEN: 1986-1995 | 00110270 / $17.99 |
| VOL. 165 – GREEN DAY | 00210343 / $17.99 |
| VOL. 166 – MODERN BLUES | 00700764 / $16.99 |
| VOL. 167 – DREAM THEATER | 00111938 / $24.99 |
| VOL. 168 – KISS | 00113421 / $17.99 |
| VOL. 169 – TAYLOR SWIFT | 00115982 / $16.99 |
| VOL. 170 – THREE DAYS GRACE | 00117337 / $16.99 |
| VOL. 171 – JAMES BROWN | 00117420 / $16.99 |
| VOL. 172 – THE DOOBIE BROTHERS | 00119670 / $16.99 |
| VOL. 173 – TRANS-SIBERIAN ORCHESTRA | 00119907 / $19.99 |
| VOL. 174 – SCORPIONS | 00122119 / $16.99 |
| VOL. 175 – MICHAEL SCHENKER | 00122127 / $17.99 |
| VOL. 176 – BLUES BREAKERS WITH JOHN MAYALL & ERIC CLAPTON | 00122132 / $19.99 |
| VOL. 177 – ALBERT KING | 00123271 / $16.99 |
| VOL. 178 – JASON MRAZ | 00124165 / $17.99 |
| VOL. 179 – RAMONES | 00127073 / $16.99 |
| VOL. 180 – BRUNO MARS | 00129706 / $16.99 |
| VOL. 181 – JACK JOHNSON | 00129854 / $16.99 |
| VOL. 182 – SOUNDGARDEN | 00138161 / $17.99 |
| VOL. 183 – BUDDY GUY | 00138240 / $17.99 |
| VOL. 184 – KENNY WAYNE SHEPHERD | 00138258 / $17.99 |
| VOL. 185 – JOE SATRIANI | 00139457 / $17.99 |
| VOL. 186 – GRATEFUL DEAD | 00139459 / $17.99 |
| VOL. 187 – JOHN DENVER | 00140839 / $17.99 |
| VOL. 188 – MÖTLEY CRÜE | 00141145 / $17.99 |
| VOL. 189 – JOHN MAYER | 00144350 / $17.99 |
| VOL. 190 – DEEP PURPLE | 00146152 / $17.99 |
| VOL. 191 – PINK FLOYD CLASSICS | 00146164 / $17.99 |
| VOL. 192 – JUDAS PRIEST | 00151352 / $17.99 |
| VOL. 193 – STEVE VAI | 00156028 / $19.99 |
| VOL. 194 – PEARL JAM | 00157925 / $17.99 |
| VOL. 195 – METALLICA: 1983-1988 | 00234291 / $19.99 |
| VOL. 196 – METALLICA: 1991-2016 | 00234292 / $19.99 |

*Prices, contents, and availability subject to change without notice.*

**HAL•LEONARD®**
www.halleonard.com

0820

173